"Modern life and thought has a centripetal force, separating into discrete units what should be held together: politics, economics, theology, metaphysics, liturgy, and history. This division of labor creates specialists who can see the units but lack focus for a larger vision ... In this substantive, readable, brief history of the relation between theology and politics, Pecknold focuses our vision by bringing together his own considerable acumen for both theology and politics. This comprehensive work shows connections that only someone of his breadth of knowledge could see. The result is a first-rate work that sets the bar for political theology."

—D. Stephen Long,
Professor of Systematic Theology,
Marquette University

"At last I have found a textbook for my undergraduate course on Christianity and Politics! Pecknold's book is brief and crystal clear, ideally suited to supplement primary source readings in an introductory class. This book helps the student grasp the sweep of Christianity's political history in a relatively few deft strokes. The broad-brush approach does not mean the book is simplistic, however. To the contrary, Pecknold's analysis is insightful, engaging, and at times contentious. Pecknold shows how theological concepts like 'mystical body' have wandered in and out of different political arrangements. In so doing, he shows students how church history and political history are not two separate subjects but one, and a fascinating one at that."

—William T. Cavanaugh,
Professor of Theology,
St. Thomas University

"If it is true that 'youth is wasted on the young,' then to restrict this so-called primer only to beginning learners or students would be wasteful in the extreme. This is a first-rate book, a serious and fascinating work on theology and politics that masquerades as a gateway resource. Yet it also succeeds as an outstanding intro-duction—readable without being simplistic, engaging key voices and eras in the long interaction between Christianity and politics. I can't wait to use this book with students, both to give them a solid grounding in key ideas and sources, as well as whetting their appetites for joining in these crucial conversations and debates. Anyone with an interest in the church and politics will benefit from this book."

—Michael Budde,
Professor of Political Science,
DePaul University

"Political theology—thinking theologically about politics and un-derstanding all political thought as first-and-last theological—is a lively field that until now has lacked a lucid and elegantly brief introduction. Pecknold's book fills that gap, and more: it makes a real theoretical contribution of its own, most notably in its treat-ment of the migration of the treatment of conscience from church to state, and the effects of that migration on the understanding of freedom, political and otherwise."

—Paul J. Griffiths,
Warren Chair of Catholic Theology,
Duke Divinity School

Christianity and Politics

Cascade Companions

The Christian theological tradition provides an embarrassment of riches: from scripture to modern scholarship, we are blessed with a vast and complex theological inheritance. And yet this feast of traditional riches is too frequently inaccessible to the general reader.

The Cascade Companions series addresses the challenge by publishing books that combine academic rigor with broad appeal and readability. They aim to introduce nonspecialist readers to that vital storehouse of authors, documents, themes, histories, arguments, and movements that comprise this heritage with brief yet compelling volumes.

Reading Augustine: A Guide to the Confessions by Jason Byassee

Conflict, Community, and Honor: 1 Peter in Social-Scientific Perspective by John H. Elliott

An Introduction to the Desert Fathers by Jason Byassee

Reading Paul by Michael J. Gorman

Theology and Culture: A Guide to the Discussion by D. Stephen Long

Reading Bonhoeffer: A Guide to His Spiritual Classics and Selected Writings on Peace by Geffrey B. Kelly

Justpeace Ethics: A Guide to Restorative Justice and Peacebuilding by Jarem Sawatsky

Creationism and the Conflict over Evolution by Tatha Wiley

Theological Interpretation of Scripture by Stephen E. Fowl

Feminism and Christianity: Questions and Answers in the Third Wave by Caryn D. Riswold

Angels, Worms, and Bogeys: The Christian Ethic of Pietism by Michelle A. Clifton-Soderstrom

Christianity and Politics

A Brief Guide to the History

C. C. Pecknold

CASCADE *Books* • Eugene, Oregon

CHRISTIANITY AND POLITICS
A Brief Guide to the History

Cascade Companions 12

Cascade Books
An Imprint of Wipf and Stock Publishers
199 W. 8th Ave., Suite 3
Eugene, OR 97401

www.wipfandstock.com

ISBN 13: 978-1-55635-242-3

Cataloging-in-Publication data:

Pecknold, C. C.

    Christianity and politics : a brief guide to the history / C. C.
Pecknold.

    xxii + 174 p. ; cm. 23 — Includes bibliographical references.

    Cascade Companions 12

    ISBN 13: 978-1-55635-242-3

    1. Christianity and politics. 2. Church and state. I. Title. II. Series.

BR115 .P7 P43 2010

Manufactured in the U.S.A.

Contents

Acknowledgments

I am happily indebted to Stephen Fowl for so many things, including the recommendation that I write this book. Special thanks also go to Fritz Bauerschmidt for his friendship and guidance at some crucial stages in my theological development. Mike Budde, in the Political Science department at DePaul University, and Steve Long, in the Theology department at Marquette, each deserves thanks for a festive summer of conversation about theology, politics, and liturgy that was funded by the Lilly Foundation, and hosted by Calvin College. William Cavanaugh read the entire manuscript and provided invaluable corrections and encouragement. These five colleagues have been extraordinarily helpful to me as I have thought about how Christianity relocates political thought, always bringing it back into relation to the City of God.

This book also benefitted from discussions with numerous students who took my course on theology and politics at Loyola, as well as those who took my course on Christianity and culture at The Catholic University of America. Stephen J. Lloyd deserves special mention amongst these students for a research project he did with me on American politics and Catholic identity. Fr. Peter Kucer gave me his invaluable philosophical, theological, and political comments on the majority of the manuscript, and made some useful suggestions with regard

x   *Acknowledgments*

to the conscience. Robert Koerpel also provided helpful feedback on parts of the manuscript. Above all, Allison Ralph, my indefatigable Research Assistant at Catholic University, deserves more than my thanks. Without her historical acumen and editorial discipline this book would have been diminished. Though none of these people are responsible for the shortcomings of this guide, they most certainly have made it a pleasure to read to write, and hopefully more enjoyable to read.

Parts of this book were given as lectures across the country, at Loyola University Maryland, DePaul University in Chicago, the Church of the Servant King in Eugene, Oregon, and at The Catholic University of America in Washington, DC, where the work was completed. I am grateful to each of these institutions for their support. Parts of the introduction, as well as parts of chapters 4 and 8 include substantially revised portions of the argument made in my article "Migrations of the Host: Fugitive Democracy and the *Corpus Mysticum*," in *Political Theology* 18:1 (2010). Parts of chapter 9 were first prepared as talks on Pope Benedict's encyclical, *Caritas in Veritate*, which I gave at both Catholic University of America and at Loyola University Maryland.

I am especially grateful to my Dean at Catholic University, Msgr. Kevin W. Irwin, for his inspiring vision for the School of Theology and Religious Studies, the sacrifices he makes to do such work, and for his steadfast encouragement to junior scholars such as myself. Indeed, all of my colleagues at Catholic have been supportive, as well as intellectually stimulating conversation partners, especially Joshua Benson, Joseph Capizzi, Michael Gorman, Bill Loewe, William Mattison, and Christopher Ruddy.

Msgrs. Paul McPartlan and Robert Sokolowski, as well as the Rev. Dr. Brian Johnstone, deserve thanks for a stimulating presentation on the recent work on natural law done by the International Theological Commission that helped me prepare the final chapter. At Cascade Books, Jim Tedrick and Charlie Collier have encouraged and assisted me in more ways than I can count. It is exciting to see a relatively new press excel in a crowded field, especially one with such a strong ecumenical vision. They are excellent because they are good theologians before they are good editors and publishers. I am grateful that they are both.

Thanks finally go to my wife Sara and my son William, especially for sacrificing weekend and vacation time that we might have otherwise spent happily together. My Mom and Dad deserve thanks, as do my in-laws for all their generous support. I am doubly grateful for my grandparents, Cliff and Rita Pecknold. Their constant love and presence, regardless of geographical distance, have always made me happy, rooted, and relaxed. My grandparents allowed me free reign of their Fidalgo Island home for two weeks of concentrated work on an early version of this manuscript—a much-needed summer respite from the humidity of the other Washington. The rough-hewn, verdant, and nautical beauty of the Pacific Northwest was an inspiration as I thought about the politics of participation in God's own city.

The Feast of the Epiphany, 2010
Washington, DC

Introduction

It is not simply for rhetorical flourish that politicians in America so regularly invoke God's blessings on the country. It is because the relatively new form of power we call the nation-state arose out of a Western political imagination steeped in Christianity. This book argues that a new construction of politics arose in the modern period, a politics actively engaged in re-constructing a Christianity that could serve the purposes of national politics. Modern politics did not simply "secularize" the world—the last five centuries of modern politics have constructed a purpose-built faith that scholars have come to call "civil religion." In the process, the modern relationship of Christianity and politics has been reformed, and at times deformed, to serve uniform ends.

We are not, however, accustomed to noticing how the relationship has been formed. We pause only for a moment to consider that prayer opens both legislative houses in America each day, or that the Queen of England formally appoints the Archbishop of Canterbury. We do not give much thought to the invocation of God's blessing in every political speech (as if the use of the divine name justifies the human claim to authority). American civil religion is not so hidden from our view, but we have become unaccustomed to noticing it. How much of our year—not only the Fourth of July, but from Labor Day to Memorial Day as well—is shaped around holidays intended to sacralize the nation in one way or another? When we place hand on heart to say the pledge of allegiance, what sort of act is this? What sort of allegiance are we giving to what sort of political body? What sort of solidarity do we feel when, especially after some great national sacrifice (soldiers coming home from war, or an event like 9/11), we see the flag hung on every porch, every storefront window, and every suit lapel? Is the flag like a sacrament of our national communion with one another? Why do we make theological claims on our national currency? Why does trusting God become a recipe for trust in our currency markets? What claims about human beings and human community are being made in such small acts? This book offers a guide through a history that will be helpful to anyone who has ever entertained such questions.

Why a Brief Guide to the History?

People often ask me to recommend a good, relatively brief history of Christianity and politics. It is a difficult question to answer. There are extraordinary, magisterial, but difficult and massive tomes, like Sheldon Wolin's *Politics and Vision*, which are hard to recommend to the casual reader (though more will be said about Wolin below). There are books that are much easier to recommend—like Hugo Rahner's *Church and State in Early Christianity*, John Bossy's *Christianity and the West 1400–1700*, J. N. Figgis's *Political Thought from Gerson to Grotius: 1414–1625*, or William T. Cavanaugh's *Theopolitical Imagination*. These books are eminently readable and learned without being footnoted to the gills, and though they often cover only a portion of Christian history, the scholar would prefer a wise selection of these shorter, more focused books than one long, door-stop of a tome. At the end of the conversation, however, I realize that no recommendation has been made for the kind of book being sought. This book attempts to be the "brief guide" to the history of Christianity and politics that readers have asked for. This book, neither a massive tome nor a specialized study, falls into the category of the "very short introduction." As such it can serve both the casual reader looking for such a guide and the undergraduate or graduate student who may find such a supplement helpful to their work with primary source material.

The nine chapters of this book provide a broad-brush sketch of a complex history that runs from the classical period to the early church, from the organic unity of medieval society to the disunity of early modern Christendom, and from the national divisions to the secularizing, liberal-democratic cultures generated by modern nation-state formation. While we have many historical accounts that come primarily from the perspective of political philosophy, and some that come primarily from the perspective of political theology or church history, we have hardly any that avoid what historian Christopher Dawson called "the artificial separation between ecclesiastical and political history."[1] We do have a few like these, and this brief guide is self-consciously written in the tradition of those scholars who have examined the history of both theology and politics together. For example, Anglican and Catholic scholars such as John Neville Figgis and Christopher Dawson studiously avoided in their work that "artificial separation" between

1. Dawson, *Dividing of Christendom,* 27.

Christianity and politics. Each in their own way attempted to remove the "and" from "Christianity and politics," and this book does the same by differentiating a Christian politics from the Christianity that was constructed to serve the needs of modern national, international, and global politics. Our choice is not between Christianity *or* politics, nor is it between *transcendence* or *immanence*, nor do we intend to collapse any of these distinctions. Our concern is to understand the relationship between Christianity and politics throughout history, and to make some helpful distinctions in the process.

Faith and Political Reason: Conversing with Henri de Lubac and Sheldon Wolin

In addition to writers like Figgis and Dawson, the book is also inspired by those who are more firmly in church history or political history respectively, namely the Catholic theologian Henri Cardinal de Lubac and the political historian and democratic theorist, Sheldon Wolin. In 2004, Wolin published an expanded edition of *Politics and Vision*, nearly doubling the size of his classic 1960 edition, and building upon his original thesis. I have argued elsewhere that Wolin's vast, ambitious critique of liberal democracy— in which he counsels the decoupling of democracy and liberalism, and offers a constructive argument for "fugitive democracy"—significantly depend on an argument made by Henri de Lubac concerning the meaning of the "mystical body" of Christ (*corpus mysticum*) in the patristic, medieval, and early modern periods.[2] In light of the importance of these two thinkers for the argument made in this book, it is worth briefly recounting de Lubac's argument and Wolin's use of it. It contributes something important to the way we will read the history. For at the heart of this book is really a conversation between faith and political reason, and specifically between Sheldon Wolin and Henri de Lubac. Let me explain the nature of this conversation before we begin.

De Lubac had puzzled over nineteenth-century ecclesial documents that consistently referred to the Catholic Church as "one mystical body," as the *corpus mysticum*. He set out to find where this term came from. He could trace the use of the word for the church back to the Papal bull *Unam Sanctam* (1302), and even as far back as the ninth century, but no further. Why was the church referred to as a mystical body for only the late medieval and modern periods? De Lubac wondered how the term came into usage. His genealogical study of the term revealed that a kind of inversion had taken place by incremental degrees, "slowly, imperceptibly a disassociation began to occur."[3] By tracing the use of the term in the early church, de Lubac found that the meaning of *corpus mysticum* had significantly changed by the medieval period. The meaning of the term had changed from its particular liturgical use in the early church, where it referred specifically to the sacrament of the Eucharist, to the broader, more generalized socio-political usage that had settled by the mid-twelfth century, where it referred to the church, and also Christian society as a whole, as a mystical body. Where "mystical body" once referred to Christ's

2. For a fuller account of Wolin's dependence on de Lubac, see my essay, "Migrations of the Host."

3. De Lubac, *Corpus Mysticum*, 96.

mystical or sacramental presence in the bread and wine
of the Eucharist, which was constitutive of the church, the
later use of the term referred almost exclusively to a more
abstracted view of the church-society as the mystical body.
These medieval shifts in terminological usage ushered in a
new modern formulation, which remained in use until the
twentieth century, and explained the nineteenth-century
expressions he had originally questioned.

On one level, de Lubac had answered his own basic
question as to why *corpus mysticum* was not used to describe the church until the medieval period. Though on
another level, his work raised more questions than it could
answer. For example, de Lubac's study raised one interesting question that the political theorist Sheldon Wolin found
especially important. If the idea of the "mystical body"
could migrate from the Eucharist to the church to society,
where else could it migrate? If the very power and presence
of God were somehow communicated through these two
words in the early Christian community, what would happen if the idea of the "mystical body" migrated *beyond* the
Christian community—for example, what if the idea of the
corpus mysticum migrated to the modern nation-state or
the economy? Wolin's work amplifies these latent implications in Henri de Lubac's study, and the influence of these
thinkers on my understanding of the history will be evident
in these pages. That is, my own thinking about Christianity
and politics has been shaped by bringing theology and
political reason into dialogue precisely in the relations between Wolin and de Lubac. Other dialogues are needed, but
this one provides us with a start.

The narrative that both thinkers attend to is vast, and the argument that emerges from it can only be suggested in a book of this nature. In case the strands of the argument that emerges from this narrative are missed along the way, I want to make explicit from the outset the argument that runs throughout this brief guide to the discussion about Christianity and politics. There are five basic claims that are being made in these pages:

1. The Western political imagination "borrows" Christian ideas about *time and community*, especially ideas about the purposefulness of history, communal salvation, and hope for the future.

2. The development of Christian thinking about the Eucharist as the "mystical body of Christ" that mysteriously unites a human society to God opens the way for early nation-states to conceive of politics in "mystical" terms, and that this *borrowed mysticism in politics gives rise to nationalism* as a tool for collecting human allegiances into a new unified political body called the nation-state, even as it aided the disunity of the church through the reformation and post-reformation unfolding of Europe.

3. One of the corollaries of this process was the severing of the medieval understanding of how the conscience was formed in the Christian community, and so we trace how *the conscience slowly became detached from one community, and was re-attached to another.* In the process, however, the conscience became unhinged, and came to be seen as a limit on human freedom

rather than as a basis for it. Thus a new order for human freedom is imagined in the early modern period.

4. The rise and fall of the conscience and the migrations of the "mystical body" from the Eucharist to the church to the society, to the state and market also made it possible *to transfer the idea of the mystical body to liberal democracy.* The unifying ideal of "liberal democracy," constructed on the back of a Christian "social imaginary" that understood social unity and redemption in mystical terms, can distort the Christian vision of social unity and redemption, as much as it can mystify and sacralize the idea of democracy itself.

5. Rather than posit how Christianity is either resistant to politics, or embracing of it, my argument is that we have to think in more complex ways about the relation of Christianity and politics, the relation between faith and political reason. A church conceived as unified, holy, apostolic, and "full of grace" provides a contrast to other ways of imagining how humanity is gathered, but this does not mean that the church is known merely by these contrasts. Rather, *the freedom of the church catholic consists precisely in having encountered the truth in Christ*; the church is constituted in freedom precisely to the extent that it is formed by the communion of God's triune love for humanity. The conclusion is that the politics that truly liberates humanity is the politics that is truthfully ordered to the city of God.

These are strands of a larger, more complex argument that I am not alone in making. A very short introduction such as this one can only hint at such an argument. We must necessarily pass over many historical details and complexities. My hope is that readers who know more will be patient with the lacunae, and readers who know less will realize that it is precisely because the truth is so complex that so few books like this one exist. Nevertheless the argument can be suggested, and it seems important to have pointed this out to readers before beginning.

Finally, as noted earlier, the book is designed to be a supplement to primary texts, a "guide" that can point out certain pathways but cannot replace the more careful historical, political, and theological readings required to properly understand the relationship between Christianity and politics. As I taught the course upon which this book is based, students frequently had reason to disagree with certain points that this author or another had made, and that was always when the discussion became most interesting and instructive. At times the book might make the church appear a little too innocent, and "elite actors" a little too conspiratorial. The truth is messier than this—the two cities are, after all, commingled, only to be separated at the end of time. The migrations of "mystical body" were more often failures of the Christian imagination than they were part of some grand conspiracy. However, granting all my caveats, what students have found useful was having a guide that points to some key events in history when the relationship between Christianity and politics changed, made us sensitive to questions about who had the most to gain from the changes, and put us in a better position to understand our current situation. In the end the book asks us all to rethink and critically reevaluate the relationship between Christianity and politics.

It is to my former students at Loyola University Maryland and to my current students at The Catholic University of America that this book is dedicated. This is their book as much as it is mine.

ONE

The Western Political Imagination

Politics was once the highest form of community imaginable. As Aristotle famously said, "man is born for citizenship."[1] Rooted in the formation of the Hellenistic city-state, the *polis*, classical thinkers believed that the city was the common good, and politics was the "master art" or "master science" in search of this shared good. Politics was a comprehensive philosophical, religious, and moral endeavor. Whatever served this highest good was what was considered virtuous. And yet, for all such grand talk of a comprehensive vision of the good life together, Aristotle could not have imagined the scale of geo-politics today. The "public thing" (*politeia*) for Athenians like Aristotle was neither national nor global. The Western political imagination begins not with the image of a vast empire but with the image of citizens participating intimately in the life of a relatively small city: Athens. Yet Athens is only the beginning. The Athenian vision shaped the Roman world, and Rome in turn shaped the political imagination of Europe.

1. Aristotle *Nichomachean Ethics*, 1.7.1097b11.

In this opening chapter we examine the origins of the Western political imagination, from Athens to Rome, as a story of the rise and fall of politics before the advent of Christ. As we shall see, for both Athens and Rome politics was inseparable from both theology and virtue. Long before the rise of a church that would change the way we think about politics and theology alike, the Western political imagination was unremittingly theo-political.

THEO-POLITICAL VISIONS IN ATHENS

For the greatest of Athenian minds, Plato and Aristotle, politics was not the debased affair that we often consider it to be today—it was the highest good and the whole purpose of community rather than a side show to economic and domestic life. Politics embodied "the common good" that all were to have a share in. Its virtues were not arbitrary but were given by the gods as necessary for the flourishing of the community. Thus the political philosopher had a kind of "religious" function insofar as religion is understood as the glue that binds a community together, uniting a people to the good, the true, and the beautiful. For the Athenian, all religion was civil religion. The political theorist aimed at a comprehensive vision for the good ordering of the whole society in a way that observed no neat separation between theology, politics, and ethics. Since politics was a gift of the gods, it was also meant to be the realm of virtue, the concrete manifestation of goodness itself.

When looking at the history of Athens we can see that their high ideals of political wisdom did not really measure up to the reality. Women and slaves were not considered citizens of Athens, and thus they were not full participants in the realm of virtue. In addition, Athenian politics was often limited by being the politics of a warrior people. Athens had impressive military capabilities that helped them to continually expand its economic and political influence, which in turn meant an expansion of Athens that made a fully participatory citizenry more and more difficult. Its virtues became the ones needed for war. Wisdom, Justice, Fortitude, Temperance, and Prudence were the virtues needed for battle just as much as they were the virtues underpinning Athenian laws, Athenian families, and a strong economy. Justice was what a warrior cried as he charged into battle with the courage to kill or be killed for the sake of Athens; but by what standard could the goodness of such virtues be judged? The Athenian slave might have been first to suggest that what seems to be for the good of Athens may be neither good, nor true, nor beautiful.

Classical thinkers were not blind to these moral questions of political transcendence. They believed that the true end and purpose of human beings was political. Aristotle even defined the human being as "the political animal."[2] Politics is what made us different than all the other animals. Nothing could be more important than one's vision of politics, but how did such thinkers believe we became political animals? Where did that intellectual horizon come from that enabled us to have a vision of the common good? The answer to that question turns out to be theological, albeit a theology that will inevitably seem strange to us.

Consider the creation myth that Plato records in Protagoras's response to Socrates questioning whether vir-

2. Aristotle, *The Politics*, 1.2.1253a9.

tue can be taught, debating the very possibility of political virtue, harmony, balance, peace, and order. Protagoras begins, "Once upon a time there were gods only, and no mortal creatures. But when the time came that these also should be created, the gods fashioned them out of earth and fire."[3] However, Protagoras believes that in creating human beings out of earth and fire, the gods did not give them sufficient wisdom. Man had been given wisdom enough to survive, but "political wisdom he had not."[4] Human beings apparently lacked the practical reason necessary to care for those goods shared in common. As the myth goes, this became evident as these first humans, who were originally dispersed, began to gather in cities out of self-preservation and mutual protection from "wild beasts." However, because they still lacked political wisdom these primitive cities erupted in violence, and thus threatened to reduce humanity to a state of savage nature. In other words, the gods' failure to give humans sufficient wisdom also threatened to reduce human beings to mere animals rather than political ones, but the gods will make amends. As Protagoras (or rather Plato) tells the story,

> Zeus feared that the entire race would be exterminated, and so he sent Hermes to them, bearing reverence and justice to be the ordering principles of cities and the bonds of friendship and conciliation.[5]

3. Plato, *Works of Plato*, 209.
4. Ibid.
5. Ibid. Also cited in Wolin, *Politics and Vision*, 10–11.

Hermes questions Zeus about how these ordering principles and bonds should be distributed, whether they were to
be endowed to the elite, or to all humanity. Should Hermes
give reverence and justice to "a favored few only . . . or shall
I give them to all?" Zeus answers sharply, and dramatically:
"To all."

In simple religious terms, the highest of all Greek
gods, Zeus, gives voice to the democratic political vision of
Athens:

> I should like them all to have a share; for cities
> cannot exist, if a few only share in the virtues, as
> in the arts. And further, make a law by my order,
> that he who has no part in reverence and justice
> shall be put to death, for he is a plague of the
> State.[6]

The divine command here is a radically participatory
one. Indeed, the consequences for non-participation are
dramatically stressed to underscore the point. Protagoras
then argues that all people are thus capable of political
virtue, that human beings are capable of learning to be
political by dint of a divine gift (in this case, one given "by
Zeus"). He admits that it's not easy; it requires study, exercise, and teaching. Politics doesn't just happen naturally,
though it can be learned. It can be achieved. It is learned
through participation in the virtues ("justice and temperance and holiness") of a particular city, and it is achieved
by human effort.

What we see in this myth are some fundamental elements that help to form "the Western political imagination."
We see the importance of the civic virtues, but equally im-

---

6. Plato, *Works of Plato*, 210.

portantly we see theology at its core—religion and politics not only went together but were impossible to separate. Politics was not something discreet, separable from the rest of life. It named "the whole" in a way that our use of the word today does not, which alone should give us pause. Though sometimes we have the bad habit of ascribing politics to lots of "parts" (identity politics, family politics, workplace politics, nation-state politics, international politics), we no longer think of politics as something necessarily comprehensive and coherent. We think of it as ubiquitous to be sure, but also fragmented, arbitrary, and partial. It is important to recognize that this was not how Athenians saw politics at all.

As we have seen, Athenians understood politics as participation in the common good. To be human was to be capable of the highest good given by the gods: being political through participation in the life of the polis. Nevertheless there was an internal tension to their theo-political vision. On the one hand, the divine command for full participation in the city rested on the idea that the city would be small enough to make such participation possible for all. On the other hand, if the Athenian polis was the highest good, it followed that that good ought to be spread through political expansion. Both are perfectly reasonable assumptions on their own terms, but when we see them placed together in this way, we can observe a tension that immediately puts their theology and their politics at odds. At the moment their principles give birth to cultural and political expansion, their theological commitments to participation begin to die.

Though some may have liked to keep the classical tradition securely in the storehouse of pure thought, the ideas of Socrates, Plato, and Aristotle concerning their beloved Athens were like currency that steadily declined in value the more they circulated from one culture to another, passing from one scale of political life in the city-state to that of an ever-expanding empire. Though Athens eventually fell under its own weight, its story continued in the Roman story. Rome can truly be said to be entirely dependent upon the old classical culture of the Greek-speaking peoples. It is with Rome that we see the Western political imagination at its most expansive, and also at its most impoverished with respect to political wisdom.

ROME AND THE END OF POLITICAL VISION

The virtuous ideals and the theological narratives of Greek political thought were the basis of Roman politics. Rome had developed from a city of refugees, to a Monarchy, to a great Republic, and then finally to an Empire. In the rise of Rome we can see the very same theo-political tensions we saw in Athens. We are accustomed to thinking of the Roman Empire in fairly monolithic terms, though the truth is more turbulent and the history more gradual. The Roman political experience did not begin in detached philosophical reflection about the highest good (indeed, it should be said, neither was such detachment possible for the Athenians). As legend has it, Rome began with refugees. Fleeing from fallen Troy, fugitives in search of a new city formed Rome, but their politics was firmly rooted in the past. As with the creation myth told by Protagoras, Rome too began with violence in the city. In the beginning, "political wisdom Rome had not." But rather than a creation myth, Rome had something much more akin to the biblical story of what came after creation and after the fall. Rome's own myth of origins has to do with fratricidal bloodshed.

The great Roman historian Livy names Romulus as the first king of Rome (around 753 BC). The story that all Romans believed was that he became king by killing his brother Remus with a shovel in a dispute about who the gods favored. For it was only by divine favor, or else violence, that political power could be wielded. Under Romulus, the Roman people were divided into three tribes: the Latins, the Sabines, and the Etruscans. For twenty years Romulus engaged in warfare that greatly expanded Roman territory and power. He had formed a Senate to run the affairs of Rome, on the model of the Athenian republic, but his success in warfare gave him a lust for power that quickly outstripped the Senate of any authority it had been given initially. Towards the end of Romulus's rule, the Senate could only be called by Romulus, and when it was called Senators were expected to sit in silence as his edicts were read. Not only had Romulus developed a taste for monarchy, but god-like pretensions were increasingly in evidence.

The death of Romulus is as instructive about his god-like pretensions as his life. According to Roman tradition, recorded by Plutarch and Livy, Romulus died mysteriously and his body was not found. Some suspected that the Senate had killed him. Soon, though, as Livy records the story, a few voices began to proclaim Romulus's divinity, and then an overwhelming chorus of people proclaimed him "a god, the son of a god, the King and Father of the City of Rome."[7] Thus a new political myth was born. The Athenian political vision was clearly theological, as we have seen, but the Roman political vision had related theology and politics in an entirely new way. Now a republic could become a monarchy, and a king could become a god.

Other kings would come, but kingship remained a somewhat "otherworldly" idea to those who still had a faint cultural memory of what politics once meant in Athens. The desire for a king could only be understood, ultimately, as a desire for the gods, as a longing for a politics of a wholly other order. This relation of theology and politics, expressed as their desire for a king, had the dubious advantage of giving Rome itself an "eternal" status. Rome would be the one city that abides forever. Though as we shall see, it would not always abide with kings, deified by human acclaim or not, for Rome had a second founding that is sometimes forgotten by us, but was never forgotten by ordinary Romans.

The second founding also began in violence. The faint echoes of an Athenian order in a powerless Senate had long faded, and Rome had truly become a monarchy. Just as it had asserted its own theological vision in relation to politics, it had also not forgotten about the importance of virtue. Despite a long line of corrupt Roman kings who had exploited the Roman people and exhausted the city through endless wars, the Roman people still told stories about what they valued, about what virtues they most admired in people. One very important story of such virtue was the story of a woman named Lucretia.

7. Livy *History of Rome*, I.16.

As Livy, our Roman historian, tells the story, a group
of princes and noblemen were drinking wine as they over-
saw their legions of soldier at a battle in Ardea, not far from
Rome. As they drank, they discussed which of their wives
was the most virtuous. It must seem to us a very innocuous
dispute, but it was quite serious. Despite being a very male-
oriented culture, Romans praised the virtues of women. The
domestic virtues were highly prized because the Romans
believed, much as Athenians had, that the "household" is
the basic unit of the *polis* (the old Greek word for "household" was *oikos*, and the "rule" or "law" of the household was
*oiko*nomia). In other words, the larger "economy" of the
city depended on the smaller domestic economy, and the
virtues of a woman were seen in accordance with her role
in running the household. So the argument between the
noblemen was, though fueled by wine, quite an important
discussion about whose family embodied what was politically good for Rome.

The argument escalated, with each of the men claiming
that their wife was the most noble, the most virtuous in all
of Rome. Until, finally, a man named Collatinus announced
that there was an easy way to settle their dispute. He proposed that they all get on their horses and ride into Rome,
and that the state in which they would find their wives would
display their virtues for all to see. All the men agreed and
they found each of the wives in various states of revelry and
random entertainments. Except for the wife of Collatinus
who was found hard at work at the spinning wheel, with
her servants industriously at her aid in the task of weav-
ing clothing for the family. Everyone declared that Lucretia

was the most virtuous woman in Rome, and the noble romp into town was over, or nearly so. At seeing Lucretia, Sextus Tarquinius, one of the sons of the king of Rome (Tarquin the Proud), was captured by her beauty and virtue. Livy says that at that moment he plotted to have her, "inflamed by the beauty and exemplary purity of Lucretia."[8]

Sextus Tarquinius went back to the home of Lucretia while her husband was away and was received in royal fashion. That evening, when all was dark, he went into Lucretia's room and pulled his dagger close to her chest, urging her not to say a word. He threatened to kill her and her male slave to make it look as though they were caught in an adulterous act, if she did not consent to sleep with him. Fearing the harm done to her slave, and the dishonor of a presumed adultery, Lucretia did consent. Sextus left and Lucretia sent for her husband and father. When they finally arrived, Lucretia told the two sympathetic men what had happened. Prince Sextus Tarquinius "forced from me last night by brutal violence a pleasure fatal to me, and, if you are men, fatal to him."[9] They immediately sought to comfort her, to tell her it was not her fault, but Lucretia made them swear they would avenge her. Once they had promised to avenge her, Lucretia withdrew a dagger of her own from the folds of her dress and plunged the knife into her heart. As Livy tells it, at that moment, both men let out "the death cry" as blood poured forth from her breast.

Why tell this particular story in a grand sweep of the Roman political vision? Because it is precisely here, at Lucretia's rape and suicide, that we see the beginning of

8. Ibid., I.57.
9. Ibid., I.58.

the end of monarchy in Rome. In overwhelming grief and anger, Collatinus carried the innocent, virtuous, and dead body of his beautiful wife Lucretia into the Roman forum. He laid her body in the middle of the forum and began to tell the story of Lucretia's rape as the story of how the kings had likewise corrupted Rome, just as Sextus had corrupted his wife. The rape of Lucretia became, for the Roman listeners of Collatinus's speech, a symbol of how the kings had spoiled Rome, how monarchy had taken away from Romans their very right to be "political animals." His speech over Lucretia's dead body sparked the Republican revolution. Rome would cease to be a monarchy and become, for the first time, a Republic. It is the vision of being a Republic that constitutes Rome's second founding—a founding that fits the Athenian ideals much better than the monarchy. After the royal family was banished, Rome enjoyed over five hundred years as a republic, as a *res publica*, "a public thing," or a "common good" that could be shared. As a Republic, Rome could imagine itself in certain continuity with Athens. The images of Julius Caesar being killed by Senators, made vivid for us by William Shakespeare, were images that would have recalled to Roman minds the high ideals of the Republic, and their sympathy for Caesar would have been muted by the memory of how absolutist, monarchical power had once corrupted Rome.

Ironically, Rome followed in Athens's footsteps in more ways than one. Becoming a Republic alleviated the absence of any "public thing," but, like Athens, Rome continued to expand its territories to a debilitating effect. As Sheldon Wolin has argued, it failed to deal with the political realities of extended space.[10] It ceased to be simply a city-state that could comprehend the good that was common to all, and its political philosophers failed to think about the implications of this vast expansion. In Wolin's view, Rome had forgotten Aristotle's warning that if a city-state became too large, it would not know how to practice the virtues necessary for a politics of the truly shared good—the imaginative and geographic expansion of political space paradoxically entailed a reduction of what politics had once meant.

Romans were proud of their republican revolution. It was built into their political mythology and their civic religion. They loathed thinking in terms of kingship again, but the vastness of the empire seemed to require it. At the time, the less controversial title of "emperor" seemed to enable them to maintain the Republic, but to more effectively "manage" it through a concentrated power in a very strong executive. As Rome began to come to terms with its imperial status, it increasingly understood its political claims in cosmic terms (with the emperor naturally claiming divine status). Though politics was always conceived through a fundamentally religious vision of the whole, Rome had failed to heed the founding wisdom in Protagoras's myth: that the virtues of reverence and justice, the bonds of friendship, be given to all people. As the empire grew too large, Roman politics became impotent, and the republican ideals became mere political rhetoric for totalitarian power.

Thus, political philosophy failed to deal with the political, and it retreated ever more into universal reflections that were detached from the social reality. The empire had become a procedural state that operated without any sense

10. Wolin, *Politics and Vision*, 86.

of a common good, or a divine command for participation in the life of the city. It borrowed some of Athens's rhetoric, but it lacked its political substance, and thus it was reduced to pragmatic procedures. It could hardly be said to be a true republic anymore.

At the end of the Roman political vision we can see that political philosophy had failed at every stage to think about the implications of growth and change on the political reality. As one contemporary political philosopher has put it, Rome failed to face the negative implications of concentrated power, it failed to face the attendant loss of "membership" in such a political shift, and it failed to preserve a space for the kind of systematic knowledge and vision of the whole that the political philosopher is required to know.[11]

In this brief telling of the early history of the Western political imagination, one theme predominates: decline. This is exactly how St. Augustine of Hippo narrated Roman history as well. However, in Augustine's Christian critique of this narrative, Rome had been a degenerate *polis* almost from its very beginning, founded after a violent act akin to the first fratricide of Cain and Abel. In Augustine's view, the problem wasn't the concentrated power, or the loss of membership, or the loss of a systematic vision. No, for Augustine, the problem was theological as much as it was moral and political. Roman theology was corrupt at the core, and because of this, Roman virtues were also corrupt at the core. Without a true theology, true virtue was impossible, and without true virtue, there could be no "republic"—there could be no *polis*, no genuinely public thing.

11. Wolin, *Politics and Vision*, 3–4; 86–87.

When we employ the word "politics" we must remember, then, that we have inherited the term from a long tradition of discourse. It has come to us through two millennia, many languages, and multiple cultures. The word "politics" has picked up a number of associations that we will trace along the historical itinerary of this book. However, we must remember that the word has its start in Athens and Rome, and in a certain sense, it also has a kind of end there too. For in a very real sense, the theo-political vision of Athens was very imperfectly extended to Rome, and its ideals had such mixed success. What Athenians understood by the word *politeia* had no good equivalent in Roman times; and the Western political imagination might have fallen on its sword with Rome's decline were it not for the ironic and paradoxical fact that "it fell to Christianity to revivify political thought."[12]

SUGGESTED READING:

Aristotle. *The Politics, and the Constitution of Athens*. Rev. student ed. Edited by Stephen Everson. Cambridge Texts in the History of Political Thought. Cambridge: Cambridge University Press, 1996.

Plato. *The Republic*. Translated by Tom Griffith. Edited by G. R. F. Ferrari. Cambridge Texts in the History of Political Thought. Cambridge: Cambridge University Press, 2000.

Wolin, Sheldon. *Politics and Vision: Continuity and Innovation in Western Political Thought*. Princeton: Princeton University Press, 2006.

12. Wolin, *Politics and Vision*, 86.

TWO

God's New City

In the Apostles' Creed, Jesus Christ is said to have been born of a virgin, to have suffered and died at the hands of Pontius Pilate, and most importantly, he is said to have been buried before rising again on the third day. It is powerful. The claim is that Jesus Christ has defeated not only his own death, but the power of death itself. It is difficult to say how this is political, except perhaps in some cosmic, mysterious way. Indeed, the next line of the creed states that Jesus "ascended into heaven" where he sits "at the right hand of the Father." Even to the outside observer this sounds like political transcendence rather than politics itself. Christ himself explicitly says, "My kingdom is not of this world."[1] So why is it that the church has been such a puzzle to power from the moment that Pontius Pilate faced a scourged and falsely accused "king of the Jews" in first century Palestine?

From the beginning, it seems, Christianity has been perceived as either a puzzle or a threat to politics. Why? Sometimes it has been seen as apolitical or suprapoliti-

1. John 18:36.

cal, and as such irrelevant to politics and thus foreign to
the common good. More often it has been precisely those
supernatural, mystical, and cosmic claims to rise above the
political that have proven most puzzling of all. This was
certainly the case in the first few centuries of the church.
Roman emperors in the age of martyrdom found it difficult to believe that Christian allegiance to Christ could be
higher than political allegiance to Caesar. It seemed that
the church, a kingdom not of this world, had a power as
yet unknown to earthly republics. Perhaps what "revivi-
fies" Western political thought most, after its precipitous
decline at the end of the Roman Empire, is precisely the
idea of "political transcendence." For Christianity intro-
duces a new and stunning vision of the goal or end of politics. The pattern of life lived by the early church became a
new *politeia*, a common life and a "public thing" that was
ordered not to Rome's glory, but to the glory of God. That
suddenly gave the Western political imagination new horizons and a new language for what counted as "the highest form of community imaginable." As we shall see, the
results of these new horizons are ironic, paradoxical, and
for both good and ill, they are results that have echoed and
endured through history.

Christ's plainly apocalyptic tone in claiming that this
world will soon be passing away hardly seems a recipe for
"revivifying" Western political thought. Yet there are good
reasons for why the very rejection of earthly politics initi-
ates a new politics in the world. We can get our first clue
in the clear refusal to use political force to move history in
the story of Christ's passion. Much recent New Testament

scholarship points precisely to this refusal.[2] In certain quarters of Jerusalem, Jews wanted to retake the city by force, to expel the Roman occupiers who were humiliating, even defiling, Israel. Some scholars have wondered if there were even such zealous and militant Jews amongst Jesus's own disciples. This is not an unreasonable speculation on the part of biblical scholars. Indeed, for many first century Jews, the *ekklesia* and the nation had been a single concept—the covenant between Yahweh and his chosen people had been understood, for the most part, in plainly political terms.[3] The hope of Israel, God's elect or chosen people, was the establishment of an earthly kingdom that would rule all the nations of the world. Many had hoped for the restoration of the Davidic kingdom in all of its glory. Unfortunately, the most zealous amongst the Jews had only remembered the glory of Israel, but had forgotten the painful downsides of this history; the descent of David's great kingdom into a divided monarchy plagued by civil strife, syncretism, the loss of many tribes, subjugation, and finally the dispersion of Israel and the virtual loss of its promised land. Forgetting all of this, it was perhaps the hope of some who followed Jesus that he would be their new king, the long awaited messiah—"a king of the Jews" as Pilate had it written on his cross. For those who had such expectations, Jesus of Nazareth must have been a grave disappointment, for he was not that sort of king.

Christ emphatically rejects these political aspirations, even though he does not refuse the messianic title. Christ

2. See for example, Bammel and Moule, eds., *Jesus and the Politics of His Day*.

3. See Mendels, *Rise and Fall of Jewish Nationalism*.

claimed to be the very fulfillment of Israel's hopes, and
yet Christ goes to a Roman cross precisely to reject such
a violent politics. In his death on a Roman cross, and his
subsequent resurrection, he inaugurates "a new way of being" and a politics of a different order. Jesus dramatically
refuses the way in which certain Jews would have expected
the messiah to claim power. He reveals a different kind of
messiah on the cross. It was this event, seen in the light of
the resurrection, which would cause the early Christians to
think about a new way of being human, and thus a new
way of being political. It was not that Christianity was to be
"above politics" or even "beyond politics." Now there was a
whole new language for "the highest community imaginable" that had been given by God, directed towards God,
for the redemption of the whole human race. The claim that
Jesus Christ was God incarnate, that he had been born of a
virgin, had suffered under Pontius Pilate, died on the cross,
was buried and rose again on the third day was a disclosure
that also inaugurated God's new city on earthly pilgrimage.
It meant that Christianity was now comprehensive for the
ordering of life, and that politics, as it was once understood,
was not.

Preeminently, it is the event of Christ's death and
resurrection that inaugurates this new order and forms,
in the words of Saint Paul, a new citizenship (*politeia*) and
thus a new kind of freedom.[4] The freedom was not only
a freedom from Roman politics as the "highest imaginable
community," but it was a freedom for a different conception
of community altogether, and also hope for the future. It
is worth simply stating how Christian thinking about time

4. See Phil 1:27ff.

and being can be seen as a challenge to a politics in decline. For it may be no exaggeration to claim that politics learned from Christianity nothing less than the reconfiguration of time and space.

The ancient, classical view of time, for Athenians as well as Romans, was that time was eternal. Or rather, more visually, time was conceived as "cyclical." Time was governed by *fortuna*, by fate, and was eternally "recurrent." The world could return to its original chaos at any time, and life could always "begin again," but it was never directed toward any transcendent end. Even if bursts of creativity, upheavals, and revolutions came, life was determined in the ebb and flow of fate. The recurrence of the seasons (cyclically creating, degenerating, and recreating) is the most natural way of understanding this infinite view of time, and this certainly led to a way of seeing not only time, but also space, in terms of an unending "circle of life." It led some speculative thinkers to imagine the immortality of the soul along similar lines of eternal recurrence. If history was infinite, then everything new was but the repetition of the past. The future may bring bursts of creativity, it may bring decline, but the future could not bring the genuinely new. We saw as much in the strange kind of repetition between Athenian and Roman political life.

Christians understood history differently. The future constituted a dimension of *hope*. Christ revealed a new way of being in time—a pilgrim way. God had created the world with time and was directing its history. Most importantly, Christ would "come again" to bring time as we know it to an end and to reveal the common destiny for all of redeemed humanity. Time was now understood as finite rather than infinite. Not only was time not eternal, but it was also not in the hands of fate. Because eternity had come into time with the advent of God incarnate, history is now seen to be in the hands of a purposeful and loving God. History became charged with meaning, significance, and purpose. Instead of time being "one damn thing after another," every moment of time was a unique point of a history that was being called towards God's new city. The new Christian view of time meant that history could be directed towards freedom.

This contrasted strongly with the hopelessly "caged" infinity of the cyclical view of time. It should not be surprising that such a fundamental shift in the conception of time was bound to have an influence on political thought. Because Christ had revealed the end of time, he also inaugurated a greater, transcendent horizon; the Christian life was a vision of gathering up the world through time on an epic journey towards the heavenly city. In this way, transcendence actually gave time more meaning, not less. It charged history with power, possibility, newness, and a vision for a destiny willed by God. The claims of earthly politics determined by a cyclical view of infinite time looked to be all the more fragile, "temporary," and lifeless by comparison to the claims of the new Christian community and its hopeful pilgrimage towards the end of time. The more that Christianity spread, the more its view of time spread. Far stronger than the small but growing band of Christ's pilgrim people, the political powers would soon realize that Christians, in their weakness, had access to an unimagined kind of power. However it was not only the Christian view of time that would tempt political forces. It was also the Christian view of community and the configuration of space around a transcendent, but common good.

In the previous chapter we observed that an expanding empire failed to deal with the implications of an increasingly detached political membership. It failed, in other words, to take heed of Aristotle's warning that full participation was essential to the polis. Christians, however, had a new sense of what it meant to participate in a different polis. They had at once revived the older Athenian idea of "democratic" participation in the life of the city, and transformed it through a radically new understanding of community as a communion of love with God and neighbor. Once again, Christianity revivified the Western political imagination, quite unintentionally, not by making powerful claims on politics, but simply by being itself.

Christians' new understanding of community derived from how they understood the very redemption of humanity by God in Christ. In order to be redeemed by Christ, the early church understood that a believer must have a share in Christ's redemptive body. Indeed, a full immersion in water at baptism was seen as a sacramental sign that the believer had died with Christ in her immersion, and was raised into Christ's abundant, resurrected life emerging from the baptismal waters. Since Jesus Christ was the very body of redemption, the body that could carry a people over the unbridgeable chasm of sin and death, then salvation consisted of being able to participate in Christ's body (*corpus Christi*). Participation in Christ's body not only meant that humanity was being brought into communion with God, but it also meant that each person was brought into a new relationship with their neighbors—especially those who also participated in Christ's body. It has the power to turn neighbors into friends who shared this communion of God's love.

Moreover, the Eucharist was a powerful new configuration of being itself. If baptism was entrance into this new body redeemed for true communion, then the Eucharist was sustenance that kept Christians growing into Christ's body. Indeed, the Eucharist was taken to be the mystical participation in Christ's body that had ascended into heaven. For this reason it was sometimes called the *corpus mysticum*, or the mystical body of Christ.[5] Just as Christ had invited the first disciples to eat the bread and wine of the Jewish Passover feast that symbolized Israel's freedom from bondage, the early Christians understood this same bread and wine to be Christ's redemptive body, truly and mystically present in the Eucharist. It gave Christians constant access to communion with God, and in turn, communion with one another. It enabled a view of communal participation that made Aristotle's vision look too small. From the beginning it was the Eucharist that was the sign and sacrament of this new political language. The Eucharist was the early Christians' visible sign of their invisible, mysteriously cosmic and sacramental union with God in the Body of Christ. This new form of life that gave priority to participation and communion in Christ's body made the pagan bonds of friendship and reconciliation look weak by comparison. The Eucharist was real participation in God's life, and the lives of one another, as one people in communion. It was a sense of mystical unity that crossed all ethnic borders— neither slave nor free, neither Greek nor Jew, male nor female—a unity that was not abstract, nor was it made by coercion or force. No political allegiance had ever achieved this kind of community. Both time and space were now

5. See de Lubac, *Corpus Mysticum.*

redefined terms. Meaningful participation for the whole of humanity in a true body politic had a powerful hold on the social imaginary. As was true of earlier political communities, people were willing to die for the freedoms its citizenship provided. Now, however, it was a community, and a communion, whose destiny was no city of men, but God's new city. It was a transcendent vision that not even the most expansive understanding of "empire" could have competed with.

It should be remembered that this new language for politics was perceived as a threat in powerful corners of the Roman world. The stories about early Christians martyred are all true—some coliseum martyr stories with lions and the like may sound more legendary and romantic than typically banal state violence—but it all holds up well to close historical scrutiny. Indeed, the persecutions of Christians became so common in the first few hundred years of Christianity that historians identify whole periods of persecution under the name of the emperors that ordered them (e.g., the Neronian or the Domitian persecutions, which were particularly dramatic). What is often missed about them, however, is that the early Christians were not killed for their political beliefs. They were killed simply for telling the truth and for refusing to lie. Christ was their king.

Roman authorities killed many early Christians because they would not say "Caesar is Lord" (whether this meant "king" or "God" to the Romans does not matter). They could not say "Caesar was Lord" because that was simply not true within the new language for politics they had been given in a communion that professed that "Jesus was Lord" to "the glory of God the Father."[6] They were all certainly willing, as their Lord had told them, to "render unto Caesar what is Caesar's and unto God what is God's,"[7] but none of the early Christian martyrs took Christ's words to mean that they could render the kind of allegiance to Caesar that was being asked of them, nor could they separate themselves from the communion of love they enjoyed in Christ's body. Perhaps they believed that the point of Jesus's teaching was to say that Caesar was not owed very much at all compared to what is owed to God. In any case, the comprehensive allegiance to Caesar that was being demanded made no sense; and the request to deny "Jesus as Lord" was to bear false witness to the truth of a powerful new order of reality that had given them a new horizon for their lives and their futures beyond Caesar's control.

This is why we call them "witnesses" (Gk. *martyria*, "testimony given by witnesses"). They died telling the truth under that most serious oath of one's blood. Their testimony, however, made their claims louder and more powerful precisely because it challenged the comprehensive claims of earthly politics by resisting its comprehensive claims with the truth. The early Christians were not political revolutionaries or activists in the way we think of those terms today. They did not hope for some theocratic order in time to displace the unjust regime. They spoke a different political language, had a transcendent view of time, and a new vision of participation in God's city.

The early Christians threatened the empire not by withholding their vote or by raging against Roman po-

6. Phil 2:10–11.
7. Mark 12:17.

litical sins. They simply lived a form of communal life that revealed the limits of the political order, and that was revolutionary enough. For that, and other reasons, Christians were executed in large numbers over centuries. Christians were labeled as "atheists" by Roman cultural elites because they did not believe in the Roman gods and so were seen as "destroyers of solidarity." Christians, for their part, were not preaching political anarchy or resistance to the empire. What made them threatening was that they were witnesses to a vision so much greater, a vision of an entirely new order revealed for a deeper and wider kind of "solidarity" and communal participation, not in some humanly constructed good, or some botched invention of weak gods, but in the commonwealth of the one true God's love for humanity in Christ. What made Christianity threatening was that the revolutionary communion of love between God and humanity proclaimed in the life, death, and resurrection of Christ meant that "solidarity" itself could no longer be gained by politics alone.

A great revolution had occurred for Christians, but also for Western political thought. It was a shift from thinking that the political economy was the whole order, to thinking that temporal forms of power were but small, fragile parts of a much more comprehensive, cosmic vision of the divine economy. Rome could no longer be thought of as an all-encompassing power. Certainly the Visigoths did not think of it in this way when in 410 they sacked the city, revealing not the pretensions of an "eternal city" but a weak and fragile city whose political degeneration had simply become self-evident. Put in the more typical terms of political philosophers, Christianity relativized politics and changed the

way political obligation was perceived. Meaningful doubts
about political obligation were suddenly a real possibility.
No longer governed by a choice between membership in
one political society and membership in no society at all,
the Christian enjoyed a new kind of political freedom. She
believed that she already belonged to "an outpost of heav-
en." There was no need to think in terms of "engagement"
or "disengagement" in a political society because those were
no longer the basic choices. The basic choice had already
been made by God who "elected" humanity to be redeemed
through participation in Christ's redemptive body. It is not
that Christians had no regard for other communities that
made lesser claims on their identities (the Apostle Paul
himself was happy to utilize his Roman citizenship when
it suited his mission); it just meant that only one communion was comprehensive of the common good. Such a view
could just as easily require actions that seemed supportive
of other political claims, as seemed resistant; depending on
how the Christian saw them in relation to the City of God.
On an entirely reconceived notion of political obligation, it
was not uncommon for Christians to ascetically "withdraw"
from other political communities in early Christianity, but
this was not a withdrawal from politics as such, rather it was
a more intensive engagement with it. Whether Christians
lived monastically or in the midst of city life, what they provided was a different way of thinking about human community. Now political obligation was conceived around the
idea of a communion of love in Christ's body, through whom
we are united to God and neighbor. The early Christians
understood political obligation on an entirely new, cosmic

framework that re-imagined what counted as "the whole," the *catholica*.

So when Sheldon Wolin claims that Christianity "re-vivified" politics, we must understand him in a special way. Christians made no effort to "revivify" Western politics; it was neither a rejection nor an embrace of politics that made the difference. Indeed, according to Wolin, it had nothing to do with what Christians said about politics. So what about Christianity "revivified" the Western political imagination? It was simply Christians' own way of living together in community, apart from and in the midst of the rest of society. Their new form of life—essentially a communion of love—challenged and eventually transformed the older way of thinking about political community. If the political narrative had thus far been a story of decline, reaching a kind of end in Rome's imperial expansion, then Christianity represented a new beginning for that community. The rise of Christianity as a cultural phenomenon was, however, soon embraced by politics, and in that embrace, the "Western political imagination" would be "revivified" in some rather unexpected ways. Yet wherever Christians were not careful to understand the new kind of power that God had given to the church, the political embrace of Christianity could easily become a political stranglehold that could confuse and disorient Christians about the form of life that had been given to them.

As "aliens and strangers in the world" Christians understood themselves to be on pilgrimage to the City of God.[8] By receiving the gift of redemption from sin and death, and in the grace of being born into the body of Christ through

8. 1 Pet 2:11–12.

baptism, Christians had been given a new birthright. They had received an identity, and a citizenship, that trumped allegiance to any nation, state, or empire. Their interest in the politics of other communities was at best ambivalent, not because they despised politics, but because the older understanding of politics did not make sense in light of their faith in Christ the king. Though they were to make "disciples of all nations," they also understood themselves in contrast to other communities.[9] Ironically, it was this contrast itself that pulled politics in new directions.

In the next chapter we will see what happened when the empire attempted to absorb Christianity when persecution proved a failed strategy, and how St. Augustine helped to reassert the early Christian political vision in terms of the contrast between two cities.

SUGGESTED READING:

Rahner, Hugo. *Church and State in Early Christianity*. San Francisco: Ignatius, 1992.
Lohfink, Gerhard. *Jesus and Community*. Minneapolis: Fortress, 1984.
Bammel, Ernst, and C. F. D. Moule. *Jesus and the Politics of His Day*. New York: Cambridge University Press, 1984.

9. For the self-understanding of early Christians as a "contrast-society," see Lohfink, *Jesus and Community*, 132ff.

Saint Augustine's Two Cities

Imagine the relief of the ordinary Christian who, after centuries of imperial persecution, heard rumors that the emperor had become a Christian. It had all happened so suddenly. The Emperor Constantine converted after he attributed a military victory to a vision of Christ. Shortly thereafter, the Edict of Milan, a letter circulated to all provincial governors throughout the empire in 313, officially halted the persecutions. With a Christian as emperor, Christianity was now the *de facto*, if not yet the *de jure*, civil religion of Rome.

Whether or not Constantine's conversion to Christianity was sincere, the Edict of Milan was a savvy political strategy. With the empire constantly under attack from barbarian invasions, and internal divisions threatening civil war across a vast empire, it was no longer clear what held the empire together. Roman polytheism, with its varied devotions, was quite localized and not well suited for promoting the cultural unity of an ever-expanding empire. On the other hand, monotheistic Christianity, which by some estimates had spread to nearly a quarter of the population despite being persecuted, suddenly looked useful to an emperor concerned about fragmentation. After all, where the pantheon of Roman gods was divided in a myriad of customs and devotions, Christianity appeared purpose-built for unity. By uniting the church with the empire, Constantine sought to use the Christian comprehensive vision of the cosmic whole that had formerly seemed so threatening. The church's sacred and mysterious sense of being united to God and one another could aid his own imperial effort to gather and unite an increasingly fragmented empire. In sum, Constantine would attempt to "absorb" Christianity and domesticate the church for the sake of Rome. Though the idea of a "civil religion" was nothing new, convincing all Roman people that they should replace the gods of their ancestors for this Christian God would not be easy.

In addition to the obvious benefit of bringing an end to the persecution of Christians, the empire's attempt to absorb the church had other, more dire consequences—the church became an instrument of the empire. Constantine's interest in using the church as a stabilizing influence in the empire also meant he had a political interest in maintaining the unity of the church. The ecumenical council that met at Nicaea in 325, which consolidated the agreement of the whole church around central articles of orthodox Christian faith (essentially clarifying and ratifying the authority of the Apostles' Creed), was called because Constantine required Christianity to be unified in its central doctrine. Constantine now viewed the church as part of the government, and thought it should both wield civil authority and be subject to it. From a certain angle, this "domestication" of the church can be seen as persecution by other means.

In any case, it was damaging for the church. For example, we can see that his decisions had long-lasting, problematic effects on the church in the way that the great schism of Greek and Latin speaking Christians in 1054 precisely followed Constantine's own division of the empire, with Rome as capital in the West, and Constantinople as capital in the East—evidence of how such political domestication can have a powerful, negative effect on the church.

This radical rearrangement was not an easy shift, either for the church or for broader Roman society. Many pagan Romans were worried that they had angered the Roman gods by turning to Christian monotheism. This worry ran so deep that Emperor Julian the "Apostate" was, in 361, able to gain much popular support for his reversal of Constantine's vision and return to pagan worship. His reforms struck a chord with some Romans anxious to return to the old gods of their ancestors. Julian immediately went to work on turning bishops against one another, attempting to create as much dissension within the church as possible. However, the legitimacy of Julian's rule was always in question, and his anti-Christian policies were deeply unpopular in some parts of the empire. After just two years, an assassin's arrow found its mark. Legend has it that Julian's dying words were "You have won, Galilean" (*Vicisti Galilaee*), recognizing the triumph of Christianity in the empire. Thereafter, the empire returned to the path that Constantine had set for it, so that in 380 Christianity would become the official religion of the empire under Emperor Theodosius. Now that it was clear, though, that Constantinian Christianity involved certain compromises, this reversion was not unrelievedly good news. While some Christians wanted to argue that this was

God's providential way of spreading the gospel with the help of the political order, others feared that this new arrangement meant that the church was sacrificing her true identity.

AUGUSTINE'S LIFE

St. Augustine deserves pride of place for articulating a dramatic and epic rebuttal to this absorption of church into empire. Aurelius Augustine (354–429) was born in a town called Thagaste in the North African Roman Province of Numidia, or modern-day Algeria. His mother was a pious convert to Christianity, his father a Roman pagan. Their marriage must have shown Augustine, from a very early age, the very tensions that the empire itself was experiencing on a cultural level.

His early education shows a man ambitious for political glory, and at the age of sixteen he went off to study in Carthage, becoming a master of the art of rhetoric, or persuasive speech. However, his academic success only masked a deep restlessness of spirit. Although he would have been familiar with Christianity through the attentions of his pious mother Monica, he felt himself drawn to a religious cult that was popular in Carthage called Manicheism, which taught that the world was created by two gods, one good and the other evil (a kind of Platonic heresy), believing that evil was a substance. He followed the Manichean way of life throughout much of his twenties, but was disabused of its truth through a deeper engagement with Platonic thought. At age thirty he went to Rome in pursuit of his career as a teacher of rhetoric. The spell of Manicheanism was broken by then, and he raised himself up through the intellectual heights of neo-Platonic philosophers, especially Plotinus and Porphyry. However he remained restless. He moved from Rome to take up a post teaching in the imperial city of Milan.

In Milan, Augustine found time to visit the Cathedral to listen to the Bishop Ambrose preach on Christianity as a way of life. At first he was attracted to Ambrose as a rhetorician, admiring persuasive speech whenever he heard it. However, before long Augustine became attracted to the content of what Ambrose had to say. Christianity sounded meaningful to him, its truth reached directly into his restless soul in a way that Manicheism had not, and appealed to his intellect in a more excellent way than Platonism. Famously, as Augustine sat in a Milanese garden one day, he heard some children singing *tolle lege, tolle lege*, that is, "take and read, take and read." Instead of simply hearing these words as children's nursery songs, he heard in them a divine sign to take and read Paul's letter to the Romans, which he held in his hands. As he began reading the message of Christianity as Paul had preached it more than three hundred years earlier, he says a light began to fill him. Unlike Manichean dualism, but more like Platonism, Christianity spoke only of one God—not merely the God of Christians, but the one God of all.

While Platonism had prepared him to see the truth of monotheism, neither Platonism nor Manicheism prepared him for the revelation that God would become flesh, a part of his creation. Both these had taught that the flesh, the physical, was unclean, evil or less than true good, but Christianity held a strikingly different view of matter. Rather than find matter to be evil, or God to be infinitely distant, beyond the material world, Christianity taught that this one God actually united matter to himself by becoming flesh in the man Jesus Christ. Augustine records in his *Confessions* that at that moment his soul was infused with light, the scales fell from his eyes in a flow of tears, and he recognized that this was the absolute truth. The Apostle Paul had impressed Augustine to "put on the Lord Jesus Christ." The good news of Christianity was the way of participation in God's own life in Christ whose body was not determined by sin, or decay, or an evil god, but was a body that saves, restores, heals, perfects, and elevates humanity. In that Milanese garden, Augustine was saved by hope in Christ's bodily resurrection. Augustine's life was now ordered to a vision of God that brought peace to the restless soul.[1]

Augustine was baptized into Christ's body at the Easter Vigil in the Cathedral at Milan on April 25, 387. He was thirty-two years old, and though he looked the same, his life was now different. Augustine chose to return to Africa to take monastic vows with other Christians he knew in Thagaste. After the deaths of both his mother and his son, which grieved him deeply, Augustine came out of monastic life. In a nearby seaside town called Regius Hippo, he found himself being called to become a priest in 391. His zeal for the truth of Christianity spread, and soon he was made Bishop of Hippo in 395 and actively built up the church in the North African Province of Numidia. Augustine's fame, as Bishop of Hippo, spread widely too.

It is this background that helps us to see why some people turned to Augustine—an elite Roman citizen as well as a Bishop—for help in conceiving the proper relationship

---

1. See Augustine *Confessions*, book 8.

between Rome and the church. Such an opportunity only came, however, when Rome was at her most vulnerable. The empire had been slowly weakening for decades, even centuries; as we noted in chapter 1, its over-expansion was both its great strength and its great weakness. Though imagined to be an eternal, invincible city, Rome was so vulnerable that in AD 410 the city was defenseless against an attack by Alaric and his Gothic army, mostly made up of tribes from Germany and Scythia. They devastated the city, raping, murdering, and pillaging for six terrifying, chaotic days. It seemed as though Rome, the world itself, was coming to an end.

In the wake of such violence, it occurred to some Romans that this attack was the result of angry Roman gods who were vengeful for having been displaced by the Christian God. Such popular pagan piety, which Julian the Apostate had embodied in his short tenure as emperor, had not come to terms with the exclusive claims of Christianity. These Romans began to blame the Sack of Rome on Christianity. As Augustine wrote,

> Rome was overwhelmed by an invasion of the Goths under their king Alaric and by the force of a great disaster. The worshippers of the many false gods, whom we call by the well-established name of "pagans"' attempting to attribute Rome's troubles to the Christian religion, began more sharply and bitterly than usual to blaspheme the true God.[2]

Since he was already known as the church's most articulate son, it was natural to ask him to defend Christianity from

2. Augustine *Retractions*, 2.43.1.

the charge. In responding to the accusation, Augustine had two immediate aims: to show Romans why Christianity was not to blame, and to show why Christianity was Rome's true sanctuary and hope, indeed, a very present help in its time of greatest need. In order to do this, he sought to show them why their gods failed them, and why the Christian God never would. In his first ten books, he showed his readers not only that the pagan gods never brought Rome health or happiness, either in material or spiritual terms, but that they were logically incapable of doing so. In the second half of his response, over twelve books, Augustine showed his readers why only the Christian God could save Rome. His response was a work spread over twenty-two books, written over seventeen years, and collected under the title, *The City of God Against the Pagans* (*De Civitate Dei Contra Paganos*). It is this work that revolutionized the relationship between Christianity and politics in the Latin West, and to which we now turn.

THE TWO CITIES

Augustine would have heard the reports—news of bloody streets and families broken apart by violence, perhaps even reports of people he knew slain or raped. A compassionate man, Augustine would not have been immune to the distress and fear that had left the empire in shocked disarray. The Goths had destroyed the gardens and palace of Sallust, as well as countless Roman shrines and other important imperial landmarks, though remarkably, they spared the basilicas of Saints Peter and Paul (Vatican Hill). Indeed, the churches were the only safe place for Romans to hide from the barbarian attack, and everyone recognized how unusual this was. It was virtually unthinkable for invading armies not to destroy the shrines of gods, because the gods were always seen as the protectors of the city. Destroy the shrines, and the people will no longer have access to the gods who protect the city. As Augustine notes with astonishment, the Goths did not destroy churches at all, but rather "the sacred places of the martyrs and the basilicas of the apostles . . . afforded shelter to fugitives, both Christian and pagan."[3]

As Augustine began his opening argument in book one of *The City of God*, he sought to prove to the Romans that the Visigoths' respect for the Christian God was a sign of the truth of Christianity, and that the shelter the churches provided during the attack was evidence that the church was God's sanctuary at the heart of the earthly city— indeed, Christ's Body, the church, was Rome's true protector. He argued that Rome should not blame Christianity; Romans should thank Christ for offering the only protection available during the attack. Yet Augustine knew well that his argument would need to do more than merely point to the protection that Christ had provided for Rome in his church. He would need to challenge their view of the gods, their understanding of Roman virtues, and the narrative they had lived by, not only since Rome's founding, but since the age of their Hellenistic forbearers. Indeed, Augustine argued that it should not surprise Romans at all that Rome fell by siege, or that the gods did not save her, because Troy suffered the same fate, and after all, everyone knew that the Roman gods were the gods of Hellenism too. As he would ask, why did they hope in such "conquered gods"? Against

3. Augustine *City of God*, 1.1.

the lingering view that Rome was the eternal city, the comprehensive whole around which everything was ordered, including the gods, Augustine had to show them something grander, something truer, and more comprehensive still. That grander, more comprehensive vision was the biblical story of two cities commingled in time, but destined to be separated in the end: the City of Man and the City of God.

In order to show his argument in some detail, it is worth highlighting two critiques that Augustine made of Rome, one ethical, and the other theological. The first critique depends on Rome's own understanding of what counted as virtue. He began the work telling his readers that the burden of proof is upon him to show why the Christian virtue of humility is superior to Roman virtues of pride, honor, and glory—and to show why God's city is more glorious because of such an alternative view of what counts as virtue. He knows how difficult it is to make such an argument, but he also knows that "pride goeth before destruction, and a haughty spirit before a fall."[4] Returning to Rome's founding myths, Augustine recalled the story of Lucretia and her virtue of honor as the highest of all Roman virtues. Lucretia, you will recall, embodied Roman virtue precisely because she took her life rather than suffer dishonor. Indeed, Augustine cited many examples of this tendency in Roman history—the example of many a brave general who did the same rather than face the shame of defeat; but no example would have been as powerful or as fundamental as the example of Lucretia, because it was her suicide that had given rise to Rome's freedom, to the glory of the Republic itself.

4. Prov 16:18.

However, Augustine asked his readers what sort of virtue brought self-destruction? Lucretia's rape was not her fault; she had done no wrong. She committed suicide because her culture admired this as an act in defense of their highest virtue, honor. What sort of confused culture would increase injustice to defend honor? What justice is done by suicide? His critique began not only by stating how irrational the act is, but also by pointing out that even on Rome's own terms, it should be considered illegal. Indeed, Augustine was the first Western thinker to argue that suicide is irrational, illegal, and immoral. The legal argument must have puzzled his Roman readers most, as he argued that her suicide was unwittingly against a Roman law that had declared that executing a criminal without trial was a punishable offense. Thus executing a chaste and innocent woman could make no legal sense whatsoever, but this is exactly what Lucretia did. She assigned herself a punishment for a crime she did not commit. "That highly extolled Lucretia also did away with the innocent, chaste, outraged Lucretia."[5]

Furthermore, Augustine questions what sort of virtue, and what sort of strength, leads to self-destruction? He intimated that Rome's most highly prized virtues, even its great foundation myths, were flawed at the core. Augustine argues that not only are Rome's virtues flawed, but that the Christian virtue of humility is the reason why Christian women who were raped during the Sack of Rome did not commit suicide. Augustine did not have in mind the modern notion of humility as a rhetorical strategy and an attitude (potentially a disingenuous false humility), but he

5. Augustine *City of God*, 1.19.

demonstrated "the excellence of humility" as a kind of habit that Christians practiced in the face of suffering. For where Lucretia's honor led to self-destruction, Christian humility led women to endure suffering in a way that conformed them more closely to Christ crucified. The implication was that Christian women were stronger than Roman women, and Augustine clearly saw in examples like Lucretia not only the failure of the Roman virtues, but also how the Roman virtues could lead to the self-destruction of Rome herself. To put the sharpest point to his ethical critique, Augustine argued that it was Rome's own virtues that lead to self-destruction from within. Further, just as it is irrational for Lucretia to self-destruct for the sake of Rome's virtues of honor, pride, and glory, so it is irrational for Rome to defend these virtues against Christianity. Not only have such virtues not saved Rome, they seem to do her nothing but harm.

The second critique that Augustine develops, in service of his overall attempt to fit Rome's story into a larger story of the City of God, is theological. In the middle of *The City of God*, Augustine reaches the climax of his argument against Roman polytheism. He has been at pains to show Rome that the gods have brought her no benefits whatsoever. At times he tries to point out how the best Hellenistic sources of Roman thought, especially Platonic ones, suggested that there was one God (the Logos) above all the gods. Augustine's approach is not simply to criticize, but to show his Roman readers that their own best sources point to the monotheism of Christianity. However, a crucial theological difference remained. Even when Roman theology discerned that there was one supreme Good, a god above all gods, this was never a challenge to belief in the pantheon of gods. Moreover it admitted mediating spirits who kept open communication between the gods and humanity. These spirits, or demons, Augustine argued, were neither gods nor humans. They were something in between. That meant that they could bring neither the "happiness" of the gods to humanity nor the "wretched" needs of humanity to the gods. Augustine asks, if they cannot bring human needs up to God, nor bring divine happiness down to humanity, "How can they help?"

Augustine's theological answer to his Roman readers crucially turns on their desire to be happy. He argues that what Romans should look for if they really want to be happy is "a mediator who is not only human but also divine, so that men may be brought from mortal misery to blessed immortality by the intervention of the blessed mortality of this mediator."[6] After having drawn his readers through his critique of Roman virtues, and through a critique of Roman theology—all standing in overall critique of Roman politics—he is now able to move more positively from the potential monotheism of Hellenistic wisdom, to the need for a true mediator between God and humanity. All of this serves to bring the same message to Rome that the Apostle Paul had brought to the Romans centuries earlier: the proclamation of Jesus Christ as the one true Mediator between God and man. As the prophet Micah asks, "By what means shall I reach God?" In Christ, Augustine argues, we have a mediator who can not only deliver us from every evil in this present life, but can deliver us even from the evil of death. "For the fruit of his mediation is just this: that those

6. Augustine *City of God*, 9.15.

for whose liberation he was made a mediator, should not themselves remain forever in death, even the death of the flesh."[7] It is ultimately the bodily resurrection of Christ that gives Augustine this hope, this confidence to proclaim Christ as the way to happiness and eternal life. Only by being attached to Christ (being participants in Christ's Body) can humans become attached to the Source, to the Father of creation. To put his argument succinctly, Augustine states that Romans, like all men, desire to be happy; the only way to become happy is to become united to the Source of our being, and the source of all wisdom, truth, and light. Jesus is this Light that illumines all humanity, and it is thus only by the embrace of Christ that we can become re-attached to the one true God; in Christ's Body we can receive God's grace, which expands our capacity for true virtue in the love of God and neighbor.[8]

By now we have seen the contrast clearly. Rome believed in self-sufficient virtues that lead to self-destruction; by elevating pride and honor for the sake of glory, lust for power and strength, Rome was made weak. Christianity believes in the virtue of humility that looks like weakness but enables Christians to endure suffering with Christ's strength, elevating the need for God's grace to be virtuous and happy through Christ, finding itself made strong enough to be Rome's sanctuary when Rome itself could not stand. The case against Rome had been made: the bad theology of Roman polytheism was consistent with the self-destructive effects of Rome's own scale of virtues, and both the ethical and theological problems had weakened Roman

7. Augustine *City of God*, 9.15.
8. Augustine *City of God*, 10.3.

politics from within. Rome's problem was that it had participated in a theology, a politics, and a way of life that was far
more ordered to "the City of Man" than "the City of God."
Augustine believed that Roman religion, politics, and ethics had become nearly synonymous with "the City of Man."
Nevertheless, the church was a "sanctuary" at the heart of
Rome, a sign that Roman readers ought to embrace the City
of God in her midst. Having considered these aspects of his
argument, we now have to consider Augustine's doctrine of
the two cities and its significance for the relationship between Christianity and politics.

Perhaps it will sound to some like Augustine has argued that church and empire become even more closely en-
twined. But this would be wrong. At the heart of Augustine's
reply is the great reversal of the absorption of Christianity
into the empire that had taken place since Constantine.
Constantine had wanted to bring Christianity as close to
Rome as possible. While Rome did serve the interests of the
church under Constantine in various ways (e.g., Nicaea), the
Roman Empire remained the most comprehensive whole.
The church was absorbed as the civil religion of the empire.
As was suggested earlier, this was a kind of continued persecution of the church by other means. One can imagine a
more reactionary thinker attempting to simply divorce the
church from politics as a result.[9] However, Augustine affect-
ed a very different kind of reversal—a reversal that at once
freed the church from being ordered to the state, restoring
the more ancient sense of the church as a "contrast-society,"
and set clear limits on the political order which gave it con-

9. See the discussion of Martin Luther in chapter 6 for the modern
consequences of simply divorcing Christianity and politics.

ditional autonomy and called it to a higher service. In doing so, Augustine reset the Western political imagination.

There is no "church and state" as opposed binaries for Augustine, just as there is no church in the service of empire. There is only the City of God and the City of Man, and every political order, if it is to be justly ordered, is to be ordered to God's City. He followed the New Testament vision of the church as a "contrast-society," and he looked to the whole of Israel's biblical narrative for a much more cosmic tension between two cities, between Cain and Abel, between Isaac and Ishmael, between Moses and Pharaoh, between Jerusalem and Babylon. The choice was to turn towards God or to turn away from God, as the first fallen angel did, and as Adam and Eve chose to do in the Garden of Eden. That was a choice facing every person, Christian or otherwise—and thus he saw it as a choice facing every society as well.

The entire second half of the work (Books 11–22) was dedicated to an exposition of the scriptural narrative, from Genesis to Revelation, in tracing the origins, histories, and destinies of these two cities. By narrating the two cities in this way we can see how important the Christian view of time was for Augustine. God created the world with time, and was actively involved in human history (the *saeculum*)—even uniting the world to himself in a new way and decisive way by becoming flesh in Christ—so that time might be redeemed and ordered to eternal life. Indeed, all of human history could now be seen as leading us towards Christ, as with the city of God, or away from Christ, as with the city of Man.

As well as redeeming us from caged time, we can also see how the Christian view of community was a similarly significant contrast for Augustine. He understood the church catholic as a universal community, more expansive than Rome had ever imagined, and one that called the whole human family towards its true destiny through communion with God and one another in Christ. The contrasts of Christian time and community is framed by Augustine in terms of the theological virtues of faith, hope, and love. The story of the two cities is really a narrative about contrasting faiths and contrasting hopes—contrasting *theological virtues*. But most importantly, Augustine sees the contrast in terms of the theological virtue of love. "We see then that the two cities were created by two kinds of love: the earthly city was created by self-love reaching the point of contempt for God, the Heavenly City by the love of God carried as far as contempt of self."[10] As we have seen, he saw Rome's "self-love" bringing "contempt for God," and he saw "humility" at the core of the Christian life, and thus at the core of the City of God on pilgrimage through time. In this way, we might be in a better position to understand that for Augustine humility is not only a habit that enables a Christian to face suffering, but it is also a habit that demonstrates the love of God. Augustine integrates the Christian view of time and the Christian view of community around the notion of pilgrimage (thus the church catholic is the city of God on pilgrimage), but also around contrasting theological virtues. He writes that these two cities are commingled in time, but the differences between them can be readily seen (indeed as Augustine has shown with regard to Rome):

10. Augustine *City of God*, 14.28.

> One of them, the earthly city, has created for
> herself such false gods as she wanted, from any
> source she chose—even creating them out of
> men—in order to worship them with sacrifices.
> The other city, the Heavenly City on pilgrimage in
> this world, does not create false gods. She herself
> is the creation of the true God, and she herself is
> to be his true sacrifice. Nevertheless, both cities
> alike enjoy the good things, or are afflicted with
> the adversities of this temporal state, but with a
> different faith, a different expectation, a different
> love, until they are separated by the final judg-
> ment, and each receives her own end, of which
> there is no end.[11]

Like the wheat and chaff so familiar to us from Jesus's
parable, citizens of each city will be commingled in time,
marked by different ways of life but not to be separated until Christ comes again to judge the living and the dead. The
Augustinian two-cities narrative upsets the Constantinian
model of absorption, but also any model in which the
church is somehow conceived as instrumental to the state.
Now it is not the church in the empire's pocket, but it is
the whole divine economy that stretches out as if an ever-
expanding universe, under which Rome is but one fragile
vessel being tossed about by violence, and the church is the
Ark destined for peace, ready to carry humanity to safe har-
bor, and eternal life.

Augustine identified the church with the City of God
in a careful way. He was aware that the church was filled
with sinners, some of whom who were living *secundum
hominem*, according to the City of Man rather than the City

11. Augustine *City of God*, 18.54.

of God. However, this interested him less than the church as the real, visible, and embodied presence of Christ's Body in the world, the sacramental presence of the City of God on earth as it is in heaven. In other places the church is, in the language of the Apostle Paul, an "outpost of heaven," a colony, or most frequently of all, the church is simply on pilgrimage to the Heavenly City. "Church," for Augustine, names the Body of Christ that attaches human beings who have been called into communion with God; it is a vessel that "carries" humanity to the eternal City of God, the New Jerusalem promised in the Book of Revelation.

In this narrative we can observe a kind of return to the early church in certain respects. Nearly four centuries after Christ's death and resurrection, we see the church relativizing temporal power once again, suggesting a larger political horizon, one of cosmic proportions, one in which the state, rather than encompassing the whole, serves as a modest, if still important, function in a complex world. Augustine understood the church as freeing us from the state, liberating humanity from the temptation to exceed the limits of politics and allow the state to form us as a people. In one sense, Augustine "invented" the idea that the state performs a modest ordering function in the lives of human beings; it exists to serve the common good of human society, not the other way round.

Augustine was the first to carefully distinguish between the social (higher) and the political (lower), and he insisted that the common good of Roman society was best served by those citizens who were formed by God's love, and he suggested that this could reorder Rome, and set Rome on a new trajectory. In doing so he also "invented" a new definition for the *res publica* as well. For Cicero and other Romans, a republic was defined by justice, by giving what is due. Augustine had argued that Rome was not a republic because it could not render what was due to God. Only Jesus Christ could do this, and did so on the cross. Augustine even went so far as to suggest that unless attached to God, who was the supreme good common to all, Rome was herself not a true republic at all, merely an unjust band of robbers masquerading as legitimate authority. Interestingly, Augustine presented the possibility of a different definition of republic or commonwealth, one defined by "common objects of love." He argued that common objects of love might hold Rome together, and that the better their objects of love, the more they would hold together as a people. Of course, he argued that the highest order of love, the love of God, was what would most genuinely complete their desire for true commonwealth, but in redefining politics in terms of common objects of love, he gave politics new criteria with which to judge itself.[12]

In *The City of God*, Augustine reshaped the social and political imagination for the next millennium. He did not solve every problem, but he set in motion a way of thinking about how the parts relate to a new vision of the whole. He solved the problem of the Constantinian church-state union mainly by making the Roman story a very small part of God's story of redemption in history. Augustine expanded the social horizons of his world. He set limits for politics, but he also gave politics new goals that served persons of God, and cities of God. The theoretically complex nature of medieval hierarchies, with its complementary levels

12. See Augustine *City of God*, Book 19.

oriented towards a destiny for humanity, and with its common objects of love, owes everything to his comprehensive vision.

SUGGESTED READING

Augustine. *The City of God*. Translated by Henry Bettenson. London: Penguin Classics, 2003.

O'Daly, Gerard. *Augustine's City of God: A Reader's Guide*. Oxford: Oxford University Press, 2004.

Dodaro, Robert. *Christ and the Just Society in the Thought of Augustine*. Cambridge: Cambridge University Press, 2008.

FOUR

Pope and King

Medieval Christianity follows the Augustinian "two cities" narrative with some crucial differences. Most notable
among them is the rise of papal power. The Bishop of Rome
had become not only a spiritual sign of ecclesial unity for
Christians, but the pontiff had also become a powerful
political authority. In the words of one historian, "the only
institution that ever rivaled the authority of the political order was the medieval church."[1] How did this happen? Why
do we more often associate the medieval Catholic Church
with power than with holiness? Is this the whole story? In
this chapter we examine how an unprecedented situation
for Christianity and politics arose when the Augustinian
vision of the social whole combined with the rise of papal
power. Medieval political theology is thus dominated by
the struggle to understand the proper relationship between
Pope and King.

As the early church had continued to think through
the implications of being Catholic (*Katholikos*, "accord-

1. Wolin, *Politics and Vision,* 4.

ing to the whole"), ecclesiastical authorities in the early middle ages began to imagine a more centralizing role for the papacy, one that could aid the unity of the church, indeed the unity of Christendom, in the face of vast political uncertainties in Europe. As a result, the church developed political knowledge that rivaled that of any regime in history. It is a commonplace to view this with suspicion, as a departure from early Christianity. However, we do better to try and understand this development of ecclesial power in historical perspective, keeping in mind its relation to the Augustinian narrative that had already envisioned a *respublica Christiana*, a vision of an ordered, harmonious whole in which politics was in the service of the church catholic, and not the other way round.

THE DEVELOPMENT OF PAPAL POWER AND MEDIEVAL KINGSHIP

In order to understand the history of "Christianity and politics," it is important to appreciate the extraordinary development that the papacy underwent, especially in its historical relation to other developing forms of power in the medieval world. Most importantly, we cannot understand medieval kingship without first grasping the development of papal power itself. It serves us well, then, to return to one of the key foundations for medieval reflection on the papacy.

The papacy has undergone continual development and renewal ever since Christ named St. Peter as the rock on which his pilgrim church would be built. The papal claim to historical apostolic succession from Saint Peter had closely followed Matthew's Gospel, "You are Peter and upon this

however, came at a price. To the extent that it was seen as
the subjugation of kingly powers, it also became a challenge
to political authority. The challenge would stoke the fires
of a mutual "centralizing tendency," a tendency that created
serious tensions between pope and king.

The Augustinian narrative had reframed political
power as but one modest part of an organic yet hierarchical
vision of the whole that placed the City of God as the overarching authority and the church on pilgrimage as its symbol. For Gregory, this meant that kings should not appoint
anyone to any ecclesial office. But Henry IV, despite his real
interest in reform of the church, was unwilling to part with
the rights that he thought were his by divine authority in his
own territories, such as the investiture of bishops. Gregory
believed that the papacy had been given a theological mandate to exercise political power for the greatest good, and
he strove by his reforms to maintain and strengthen those
claims. To the pope, Henry's refusal to give up the right of
investiture seemed not only like disobedience but even an
inappropriate reach for ecclesial power. It seemed to Pope
Gregory that Henry was turning away from the Christian
faith and felt the move as an attack upon the supreme rights
of his own office. When Henry IV withdrew his allegiance
from the pope in 1076, Gregory could only understand this
withdrawal of allegiance as apostasy and so excommunicated Henry. In legal and spiritual terms, Gregory made
Henry an exile in his own land.

The most famous image of the controversy immediately followed. It is the image of Henry IV, penitential, without royal regalia, clad in sackcloth, standing barefoot in the
snow at Canossa, awaiting absolution from the pope. Henry

had quickly realized that being excommunicated had put his cause at a great disadvantage and was willing to fall prostrate before Gregory and to display extreme "humility" in order to change his situation. Though Gregory doubted his sincerity, Henry's penitential pleas were met with papal absolution. The absolution that Gregory granted to Henry, however, hardly meant the end of the controversy, and both men knew that consequences would follow.

Dramatically, Gregory made Rudolf of Swabia to be an anti-king in opposition to Henry, ensuring that the battle would continue. Henry carried on, continuing his practice of investing his own bishops. This only further infuriated Gregory, who was insisting in his reforms that the church be free from royal interference in the election of bishops. The integrity of the church was at stake, and so in 1080 Gregory decided to renew the excommunication of Henry, and the king in turn withdrew his allegiance from the pope once again. Then the excommunicated king did Gregory one better: Henry installed Clement III as an anti-pope and chased Gregory out of town. When Gregory died five year later, it did not end the controversy, which continued for nearly forty more years, outliving Henry as well.

This controversy raised far more questions than it could answer. Popes would continue to invest kings with power—and kings continued to see it as their privilege to appoint bishops in their lands. But the bigger question was not squarely faced: what sort of power do pope and king have over one another? That is the question of "Christianity and politics" in the medieval era, the question of how "power and the holy" relate. Did a pope have the power to depose a king? Is that the sort of power that the pope had at his disposal? Could a king elect his own pope? That there were no easy answers to these questions at the time shows how deeply intermingled were the aspects of medieval society. There was no neat "separation of church and state." However, in the attempt to answer some of these questions, theologians and royal lawyers began developing new ideas about kingship and papal power in answer to these fundamental tensions.

THE KING'S TWO BODIES

Kings were not the only critics of Gregory's reforms. Bernard of Clairvaux was a theological critic who had concerns that the papal reforms had placed undue emphasis upon the juridical and legal aspects of the church at the expense of the spiritual and mystical understanding of the Body of Christ. Bernard asked if the reforms were true to the original vision of the papacy. Did not Gregory's reforms simply mimic royal power? Gregory had responded that just as Christ was fully human and fully divine, so the pope had two natures. In holding the keys to the kingdom of heaven, the pope also held the keys to the earthly kingdoms too. Yet such a response became tempting fodder for competitive thinking about kingship. If the pope could claim two bodies, one spiritual and divine, and another that was juridical and legal, perhaps kings could too.

After all, in a *respublica Christiana*, were not kings as well as popes divine agents of the kingdom? Did not kings also have "fully human" as well as "fully divine" responsibilities? In the wake of the investiture controversy, papacy and kingship became competitors and often emulators of each other. This is nowhere more evident than in *the doctrine of the king's two bodies*. This complicated idea asserts an abstract and mystical view of kingship and, in fact, borrowed the ecclesial metaphors having to do with the mysterious presence of Christ's body in the Eucharist that had been used in defense of papal political power.

The doctrine of the king's two bodies is especially familiar to us in the phrase "the king is dead, long live the king!" The phrase carries the idea that the king has his own natural body, which can die, and another, mysterious or supernatural body, which cannot die. The king, like the pope, would pass on a "divine right," authorized by God, to an "office," a kind of mystical body that was immortal and could perpetually rule and protect the people. The court lawyers were busy making sure that they too could harness the political power of "the mystical" for the king. The irony is that the strong assertions about the king's mystical body and his "divine rights" were the direct result of Pope Gregory insisting that kings had no such rights at all.

Cross-fertilization of thought throughout the controversy meant that the pope looked increasingly kingly, and the king looked increasingly papal. As Ernst Kantorowicz put it, the pope wore a royal crown, and the king wore papal shoes. The exchanges worked both ways over centuries, "until finally the sacerdotium had an imperial appearance and the regnum a clerical touch . . . the hierarchical apparatus of the Roman Church tended to become the perfect prototype of an absolute and rational monarchy on a mystical basis, while at the same time the State increasingly showed a tendency to become a quasi-Church or a mystical corporation on a rational basis."[5]

CHRIST'S MYSTICAL BODY

So where did things go wrong? Where did these ideas come from? We have already seen that the church had always conceived itself as Christ's Body. But how did all of this thinking about the unity of Christ's Body lead to divisions in the Christian commonwealth? For an answer, perhaps it is best to return to the work of Henri de Lubac, *Corpus Mysticum: The Eucharist and the Church in the Middle Ages.*

The Eucharist, in the first millennium of the church, was thought of as "the mystical body" or sometimes as the "sacramental body of Christ." This *corpus mysticum* was the concrete, local and sacramental bond between the historical body of Christ ascended into heaven, and the universal church, which was sometimes called "the true body" of Christ on earthly pilgrimage towards the heavenly city of God. However, if Christ's body could only be one, how could Christ's body be three: historical, mystical, and true? The answer was that the Eucharist, instituted by Christ himself, was the mysterious but real link between the historical and the true: the sacramental union of the true church with the historical body of Christ. The Eucharist was thus a cause of this communion between baptized Christians and Christ, and it was a visible sign of the grace of spiritual

5. Ernst Kantorowicz, *King's Two Bodies*, 193–94. Like Sheldon Wolin, Ernst Kantorowicz also depends on Henri de Lubac's argument in *Corpus Mysticum* for his analysis of the relationship between mysticism and medieval political development.

union of Christ and his true body the church. The source and summit of the Christian faith, indeed the foundation of the church itself, was thought to be nothing less than the Eucharist, "the mystical body" of Christ, precisely because, in Henri de Lubac's famous phrase, "the Eucharist makes the Church."[6] In this way we can see that the unity at the heart of early Christian society flowed in a concrete way from the "mystical body" of the Eucharist itself.

In the fifth century, Augustine would teach the faithful that the Eucharist was the "mystical body" of Christ, and that participation in this Eucharist makes the church. He writes,

> So if you want to understand the body of Christ, listen to the apostle telling the faithful, *You, though, are the body of Christ and its members* (1 Cor 12:27). So if it's you that are the body of Christ and its members, it's the mystery meaning you that has been placed on the lord's table; what you receive is the mystery that means you ... *Be what you can see, and receive what you are.*[7]

In Augustine's view, it is not we who make Christ's Body mystically present, incorporating him into our bodies, but it is Christ who makes humanity whole by incorporating us into himself, calling human beings into a new communion through this sacramental bond. The Eucharist is the mysterious or "sacramental" logic that knits participants into the one body of Christ ("There is one body and one Spirit...

6. De Lubac, *Corpus Mysticum*, 88.

7. Augustine, Sermon 272 in *Essential Sermons*, 318. Emphasis mine.

one Lord, one faith, one baptism, one God and Father of all,"
Eph 4:4-6).

What can be seen in the early view of *corpus mysticum*
is a tripartite view of that mysterious communion between
(1) the historical body of Christ witnessed to in Scripture,
now under (2) the veil of the sacrament of his mystical and real presence, where Christ generates (3) the one
true church in communion with God that is destined for
heaven. Christians of antiquity would not have thought of
the church catholic as the *corpus mysticum*, except by extension, but rather as the *corpus verum* (the true body). While
the church was causally related to the Eucharist as the *corpus mysticum*, it was not usually called this. Rather, the true
body of Christ was constituted by having received truth
itself in Christ. The church receives its institutional life, its
reality, its truth, as a gift precisely because it receives Christ's
mystical presence in the Eucharist as the redemptive call to
reconciliation and communion. That is to say, the Eucharist,
as the *corpus mysticum*, is the true logic of communion—
indeed the source and summit of Christian communion.
The distinctions that Christians of the first millennium
made—between Christ's historical body (ascended to heav-
en), his sacramental or mystical body (Eucharist), and his
true, ecclesial body (church)—were extremely important.
But distinctions can be made to divide as well as unite.[8]

The burden upon de Lubac was to show how the
meaning of *corpus mysticum* had slowly changed, and thus
how these distinctions changed over time (and what the
implications of such changes might be). His historical in-
vestigations led him to be critical of early medieval thinkers

8. De Lubac, *Corpus Mysticum*, 26.

who transitioned "from the *sacrament* to the *power of the sacrament* or from *visible form* to the *reality itself* so swiftly" and placed "the accent so strongly on the Church," that he believed distortions arose.[9] He saw the shifts beginning as early as the ninth century, and by the late middle ages, de Lubac argued that this language had been transformed and obscured through a new focus that inverted the terms "mystical" and "true," making the church a mystical power, and speaking of the Eucharist in a way that had the potential to separate its reality from its mystery, and also had the potential to make Eucharistic devotion more individualistic rather than more communal.

By the twelfth century, terminology once used solely for the consecrated host had begun to be used for the church, so that it was becoming far more common to call the church the *corpus mysticum*, while the Eucharist had now come to be called the *corpus verum*. The inextricable, causal, and reciprocal relationship between the Eucharist and the church shifted balance: an emphasis on the "Eucharist makes the church" gave way to an emphasis on "the church making the Eucharist." Both were true, but one came to take precedence over the other. The shift in emphasis could be demonstrated most dramatically in the way the Eucharist slowly ceased to be called the *corpus mysticum*. The Eucharist remained both mystical and realistic at once (whether called the *corpus verum* or *corpus Christi*), but it also became more a focus of individual piety; on the other hand, the gathering, communal powers of the "mystical body" shifted away from the Eucharist and migrated to the temporal authority of the institutional

9. De Lubac, *Corpus Mysticum*, 13.

church. This last point requires some explaining, as de
Lubac's point is not quite as explicit as we might like.

As the church came to terms with a new historical
situation, the earlier emphasis upon the Eucharist mystically constituting the church catholic as Christ's true body
was muted in favor of a new emphasis on the mystical
church making the Eucharist. That stressed the mystical
powers of the church as maker of communion rather than
the power of Christ's presence in the sacrament as maker of
communion. While de Lubac did not want to deny that the
church makes the Eucharist as much as the Eucharist makes
the church, he worried about this new emphasis becoming
the condition for the possibility of later ruptures. He worried that these subtle theological shifts *made it possible to
separate the mystical from the real, and the personal from the
communal.* De Lubac did not think these developments in
the use of the church's own language illegitimate in themselves, but he did think that they were problematic because
they unwittingly introduced the *possibility* of detaching the
church catholic from the source and summit of its communion and unity in the Eucharist.

Such a problem he saw at the dawning of the fourteenth century, where de Lubac observed that the language
of the mystical body had finally ceased to be used of the
Eucharist at all, and its meaning had migrated in such a
way that it was now used exclusively of the institutional
church. As the papal bull *Unam Sanctum* states, "she [the
Church] represents one sole mystical body (*corpus mysticum*) whose Head is Christ and the head of Christ is
God."[10] De Lubac's fear was that in such theological shifts

10. *Unam sanctam*, Papal Bull of His Holiness Pope Boniface VIII,
promulgated November 18, 1302. For an outstanding discussion of the

in terminology the church was also making a political shift that had been long in the making. While Augustine could speak of "two cities"—the earthly city founded in violence, and the city of God founded in peace—now it seemed there was only one city with two swords, both of which had been given to the church. As the bull states, "[I]n this Church and in its power are two swords; namely, the spiritual and the temporal . . . . the former is to be administered *for* the Church but the latter *by* the Church." That is to say, the mystical powers of the church cause and direct the material activity of the state's use of force. That makes it possible (but not necessary) for sacramental mysticism to shift from the Eucharist to the church, and from the church to the coercive activity of the state.

Now it should be easier to see what worried de Lubac. The shift in emphasis from the mystery of the sacrament of the consecrated host to the church as the mystical body also meant a transfer of power: from a church ordered around the Eucharist, to the church as a heavy concentration of institutional power directing the state. The power of the sacrament of communion had shifted from its transformative role in forming the character of Christian community to an objective view of the institutional church as a transferable mystical power. A new fusion of horizons had become the occasion for the *corpus mysticum* to migrate *from* mysterious sacrament *to* mysterious socio-political power. That made it possible to shift away from the view of the communal nature of the Eucharist towards a more individualized understanding of Eucharistic devotion, and it

authority of this bull in the fourteenth century, see Duffy, *Saints and Sinners*, 155ff.

made it possible to separate the mystical and the real, where the Eucharist was the real, and the church was the mystical. No such separation between the mystical and the real, or the personal and communal, was possible for the early church—no such abstractions were plausible.

For de Lubac, the mystery of the church is an article of faith. It is written into the Creed itself, "Credo . . . sanctum Ecclesiam Catholicam." The early Christians believed that the Holy Spirit was *in* the church, sanctifying the church, making Christians holy. The early Christians believed in the church as a supernatural reality and the sacrament of the whole communion of saints. De Lubac wrote that "to a man who lives in her mystery, she is always the city of precious stones, the Heavenly Jerusalem, the Bride of the lamb . . ."[11] Yet, de Lubac also recognized that "the dark side of the mystery is there too . . . For the unbeliever . . . the Church remains a stumbling block."[12] In his argument in *Corpus Mysticum*, de Lubac seems most worried about how the church might become a stumbling block for an unbelieving world precisely when it does not live up to being the true body of Christ. The shift in emphasis, from the sacramental reality of the Eucharist to the juridical, material power of the church appears to de Lubac to enable an unnecessary stumbling block. It need not have developed in ways that detached the historical and the real from the mystical and sacramental, nor in ways that detached the personal from the communal. Implicit in his reading of this history, however, is his assumption that the church becomes a stumbling

11. De Lubac, *Splendor of the Church*, 47.
12. Ibid.

block only when it fails to be itself—and such detachments were not the church catholic being itself.

In the next chapter, we will see how these tensions within medieval political theology escalate into the very problems that first animated de Lubac's worries about the *corpus mysticum*.

SUGGESTED READING

Duffy, Eamon. *Saints and Sinners: A History of the Popes*. New Haven: Yale University Press, 2002.

Kantorowicz, Ernst. *The King's Two Bodies: A Study of Medieval Political Theology*. Princeton: Princeton University Press, 1997.

de Lubac, Henri. *Corpus Mysticum: The Eucharist and the Church in the Middle Ages*. Translated by Gemma Simmonds CJ. London: SCM, 2006.

Miller, Maureen. *Power and the Holy in the Age of the Investiture Conflict*. New York: Bedford/St. Martin's, 2005.

Tierney, Brian. *The Crisis of Church and State 1050–1300*. Toronto: University of Toronto Press, 1988.

FIVE

Towards Hobbesian Bodies

In the last chapter we considered the importance of the "mystical body of Christ." The theology of participation in Christ as the whole of social reality had powerfully reshaped the Western political imagination. But in the early modern period, this theology of participation in the mystical body of Christ began to give way to a theology that placed much more emphasis on the formation of community through the individual will. Participation in a reality *given by God* began to give way to participation in a reality *constructed by human beings* out of the consent of individuals. This shift towards modernity began subtly, almost imperceptibly, with fourteenth-century theologians (e.g., William of Occam) who placed a much greater foundational emphasis on the freedom of the individual's will than on an ontologically prior call to a communion that might form us to truly participate in the true, the good and the beautiful. Unlike the earlier scholastic theologians, these later "nominalist" theologians found reality to be rooted less in transcendent and divinely universal ideas and more in the concrete particulars of this world of ours. As a result, a great deal of stress was placed on the autonomy of individuals, and while this contributed to humanistic thinking about human dignity and democratic freedom, it also began to erode more ancient ways of Christian thinking.

These theological shifts away from participation in Christ's body and towards the autonomy of the individual also made it possible to revise the Western political imagination once again, this time giving birth to the modern concept of the nation-state.[1] Though we have had all kinds of states in history—city-states, kingdoms, empires, feudal states, leagues, alliances—we often forget that the nation-state is the youngest of the forms of state power. It is the "modern" form of state power and it probably could not have risen without the help of some of the theological transformations we have covered. We can presume that modernity was not built in a day, and we can also presume that it did not "spring forth full-grown from the head of Galileo, Bacon, Descartes, or Hobbes but arose over a long period."[2] A number of shifts had already taken place before the sixteenth century in order for the nation-state to take shape. We have only hinted at a few of them. Nevertheless, we must turn to question the modern relationship between Christianity and politics. This chapter represents the "hinge" of the book, turning our attention towards modernity.

Three events of the sixteenth century stand out in particular: the Protestant Reformation, the wars of religion, and the formation of the nation-state. All agree that these three are related. The common story is that the Protestant

1. See Cavanaugh, *Theopolitical Imagination*, 15–20, 43–46.
2. Gillespie, *Theological Origins of Modernity*, 19.

Reformation caused the sixteenth- and seventeenth-century wars of religion and thus necessitated the early modern nation-state, which could provide a non-religious unity, a national unity that could secure the peace in a world of religious violence. That narrative should sound hauntingly familiar to us today, but we should be suspicious of it. The standard narrative presumes that nation-states have saved us from religious violence, saved us from the church.[3] Nowadays we are most likely to think that the nation-state has to save the economic ties that bind us together, but we are nevertheless still tempted by the story of the state as savior. Why? How did we come to think of the nation-state as a savior?

A growing number of political theorists have encouraged us to question this common narrative.[4] They have begun to argue that we have underestimated the role of the newly forming nation-states in the wars of religion. Some theologians, such as William Cavanaugh, have argued that these newly forming nation-states actually had a vested interest in encouraging and deepening the divisions that were emerging between Christians in the sixteenth century. In short, we have not rightly understood the full range of causes of the Reformation, the wars of religion, or the rise of the nation-state. Most especially, we have not understood the role of elite political actors manipulating the masses in order to gain comprehensive control with powerful new political tools.

3. See Cavanaugh's discussion of "state soteriology" in *Theopolitical Imagination*, 43–52.

4. See, for one example, Marx, *Faith in Nation*.

One fact that gives us a clue for re-evaluating "state agency" is that the sixteenth century was a time in which the church was being divided almost exactly along national lines.[5] As early modern nation-states formed out of monarchies, they engaged in a set of practices to consolidate state power. In the medieval model, power resided with people, with a pope or a king, not with a church or a state. States were merely the extension of the personal power exerted by a king or a lord or an emperor. States were mere instruments in the hands of powerful persons, often seen to be ordained by God. But now "the state" was getting power of its own, an independent, autonomous power formed by political elites around the idea of a nation. The trouble for these elite political actors was how to get mass allegiance to this new political form? As monarchs began centralizing their power in a new way, they harnessed growth through early capitalism to extend their empire through the spread of markets, direct rule, collection of revenues, and the provision of armed forces to protect those states and their markets. But as long as these actions were merely those of the political elites, and the masses remained allied to their typically local attachments to the family, the town, or the region—and more universally attached as "Catholics," or as "Jews," or as "Muslims"—the newly forming nation-state lacked the one thing necessary to become a *nation*, an *ethnos*, namely: it lacked *the people*. The only thing that resembled "mass political engagement" in the fifteenth century was the Catholic Mass. How could they get that kind

5. By "state agency" scholars mean the social, political, and economic actions of those who represent the state and serve its institutional and cultural ends alone.

of allegiance? In search of this kind of mass allegiance of an entire population, monarchs became heavily invested in constructing new loyalties out of older ones. This last point requires some illustration and explanation.

FERDINAND AND ISABELLA'S SPAIN

Consider one brief example, one that will be both familiar and strange to us. We have all heard of Christopher Columbus. The familiarity of his name—"In 1492 he sailed the ocean blue"—makes it difficult for us to see him as anything other than "discoverer" of America. Actually, Columbus played a part in a political invention larger than the discovery of America. He played a part in the highly complex formation of early nation-states. He was sent by King Ferdinand and Queen Isabella of Spain as part of a great plan to construct a new, unified, centralized Spanish state. The generous sponsorship of Columbus's extravagant undertaking was a sign of the Spanish Monarchs' power, clout, and authority.

Consider how the Italian political philosopher Niccolo Machiavelli (who we will examine in greater detail in the next chapter) explained the King of Spain's exertion of a new kind of power:

> Nothing makes a prince more esteemed than great undertakings and showing himself to be extraordinary. In our own times we have Ferdinand of Aragon, the present King of Spain. This man can be called almost *a new prince*, since from being a weak ruler, through fame and glory *he became the first king of Christendom* . . . He was able to maintain armies with money from the Church

> and the people . . . *always employing religion for*
> *his own purposes.*[6]

Machiavelli notes that Ferdinand looks like a new *kind* of prince. And perhaps to our great surprise, he is seen to be "the first king of Christendom." We often think of Christendom as medieval, but here at the dawn of the early modern state, we find that "Christendom" is a new idea "employing religion" for its own purposes. "Christendom," for Machiavelli, and clearly for Ferdinand, means Christianity in the service of the Spanish state. Instead of the Augustinian notion of the state serving the interests of Christianity, the "church and the people" are now seen as useful to the state.

So it should not come as a surprise that in a single year in Spain we can see the early nation-state formation at work. Far from the standard account, in which nations emerge as a more inclusive political order, what we actually see are the exclusionary origins of the early nation-state. We can also see the mechanisms through which early modern nation-states were able to transfer and captivate popular allegiances (as Machiavelli also notes, these new princes "kept the minds of [their] subjects surprised, amazed, and occupied with their outcome").[7]

When King Ferdinand and Queen Isabella woke up on New Year's Day in 1492 and heard the report that Christian forces had finally captured Granada, they knew that their project could begin in earnest. Capturing Granada completed the protracted battle to win back Spain from the Moors, that is, the Muslims. That was the first act of 1492

---

6. Machiavelli, *The Prince*, 76. Emphasis mine.
7. Ibid.

worth noting. The second act, only a few months later in March of that year was a royal decree to expel the Jews, thus bringing the Inquisition to its climax. The first two acts show us at least one early nation-state being formed on the basis of the state exclusion of religion, and the use of one religion to secure national unity—namely Christianity. The third act is the printing of the vernacular grammar book in Spain by royal mandate. The literature on nations and nationalism has nearly exhausted the insight that language is a key factor in the formation of a national identity; but Ferdinand and Isabella knew it intuitively. The use of print media to homogenize the Spanish language, which was filled with different dialects and thus allegiances, was an important political act for constructing the political imagination of the newly forming Spanish nation. The fourth act is the one we are most familiar with. In the early summer of 1492 Christopher Columbus set out on his voyage to discover a western route to India on Ferdinand and Isabella's tab. This, of course, corresponds to what we know about the importance of early capitalism in the formation of nation-states. It also shows us that the nation-state began projecting itself globally from its very beginning.

So what we can see here, in the first six months of 1492 in Spain is a new, consolidating Spanish state, which had:

1. expelled its Moorish rulers;

2. developed religious unity of a nationalistic Christianity through the religious exclusion of Jews and Muslims;

3. spread linguistic homogeneity through education; and

4. began to project itself globally through capital expansion.[8]

Stories like this can be multiplied in different ways, with different implications across sixteenth-century Europe, and these new centripetal movements can be seen before the key events of the Protestant Reformation, which began in earnest in 1517 (a generation *after* Spain flexed its national imagination). Machiavelli, as we shall see, was describing as much as he was prescribing the new power that was co-alescing around the idea of nation-state.

In many of them we see the problem the elites have in securing mass allegiance for these new collectivities called nations. Early nation-state-building often provoked local resistances where loyalties were differently configured. They needed to cultivate mass allegiance through some collective sentiment, something akin to faith.

The standard narrative is that politics gets de-theolo-gized in the sixteenth century—where Luther de-politicizes theology and Machiavelli de-theologizes politics—but it is really truer to say that politics gets re-theologized, with nationalism becoming the political religion that helps the state to secure its legitimacy.

The state required the masses to put their faith in the nation, and they used religious faith to do this. As Anthony Marx writes, the "emerging religious tensions" of the six-teenth century were "manipulated or aggravated by elites eager to use emerging passions of faith as a basis for build-ing their authority or challenging that of others."[9] In a simi-

8. Marx, *Faith in Nation*, chapter 1.
9. Ibid.

lar vein, William Cavanaugh asks, "If the struggle between state-building elites and other powers like the church pre-dates the Reformation by at least a century . . . is it possible that the state-building process is not simply the solution but the contributing cause of the violence of the sixteenth and seventeenth centuries?"[10]

By the time of the Reformation we can see faith be-coming politicized in a new way, in a way that was highly important for the early nation-building process. Christian faith, especially, was becoming the scaffolding for building and bounding national unity . . . and as ecclesial divisions developed, they actually aided this process—in fact, the early nation-states found that the divisions became highly effective tools for a new selective and secular form of alle-giance called nationalism, embracing religious sectarianism as a powerful instrument for securing its own cohesion. By exploiting the internal politics of the church, the states both help to ensure Christian division and transfer the powerful Christian idea of a people united in the mystical body of Christ to a new conception of mystical unity in the idea of the nation.

This is not to suggest that the ecclesial divisions of the sixteenth century (the Protestant Reformations) are the fault of early nation-state formation or "conspiratorial elites" who would be its agents. The reasons for ecclesial division are first-and-last theological and have much to do with the way in which the church catholic began to think of itself in increasingly abstractive degrees as the mystical body of Christ rather than in more concrete expressions of a communal identity gathered in the Eucharist as the

10. Cavanaugh, *Myth of Religious Violence*, 141.

mystical body of Christ. In this sense, the divisions are a consequence of the failure of the Christian imagination to be faithful. Nevertheless, the way we conceive of the kind of state we now inhabit owes something to the way in which elites (nearly all of whom, it must be said, were *Christian* elites) constructed new popular allegiances out of the Catholic identity in the sixteenth century.

Prior to these shifts, social unity and collective sentiment was, politically speaking, radically local, and it was only the church that held a diverse people together. However, the idea of a "mystical unity"—a diverse humanity gathered together for meaningful participation in the Body of Christ—was a tremendously useful idea for these elites invested in early nation-state building. They needed to construct a national identity out of various local ones, and they needed powerful ideas to mobilize the masses.

TOWARDS HOBBESIAN BODIES

So why do I suggest that we now think about Ferdinand and Isabella, or Luther and Machiavelli, in terms of a later thinker like Hobbes? Surely it is anachronistic to think of such figures as promoting, or moving us "towards Hobbesian bodies," regardless of how important Hobbes may be for understanding modern political thought. Yet if we can put anachronistic worries to one side, we can also see that Hobbes was not only prescribing what was necessary for England, but he was *describing* what he had already observed all across the European Continent in the several tours that he made prior to 1640. In one sense, we can best understand the sixteenth century, and the change it represents for the relationship between Christianity and politics, by looking ahead to Hobbes as one who describes in retrospect what we are about to examine in prospect. We will examine Hobbes again in chapter seven, but it is important to anticipate him as we study the transition from the medieval to the modern.

Thomas Hobbes's most famous work, *Leviathan,* was written in 1651 at the end of bloody and chaotic civil wars in England, and it offered a vision of how to restore peace and tranquility in troubled times. It is often said that Hobbes's *Leviathan* gives us a window on his time, but as we have said, he also gives us a window on a political model that had *already emerged*, a new model for the relation of Christianity and politics that he was articulating for an English audience in the seventeenth century. What we should especially notice is the *theological* change that has occurred.

This change is strikingly apparent if we pay careful attention to the image of the Sovereign (Leviathan) that appeared as a woodcut on the first edition of his 1651 publication. If we look closely, we will see that this image perfectly represents his view that human nature is violent, and that the "natural" conflict of humanity can only be averted if everyone makes a pact, gives the consent of their will, gives up some of their individual freedom to a sovereign power in order to enforce laws that will promote peace. The image is headed by a scriptural text, from Job 41:24: "there is no power above the earth which compares to you." Under the scriptural text there is the sovereign king, crowned, with a sword in his right hand, and what could be either a scepter (royal) or a crosier (ecclesiastical) in his left hand. The viewer can see the body of the sovereign from the waist up, and on close inspection the Sovereign is clothed or constituted by hundreds of tiny people. It is a striking and unexpected image to see one human being made up of hundreds of others, but there it is in its entirely bizarre seventeenth-century splendor. On closer inspection still, the viewer of the woodcut sees only the backs of the tiny bodies of the people. In other words, all of the bodies are

facing Leviathan. It is the image one would have had walking into a local parish and seeing the backs of the worshippers facing Christ on the cross. The body politic is in perfect obedience to the Sovereign, an obedience that people would have learned first in church, now being transferred to, in Hobbesian terms, "a mortal god."

Leviathan also appears to be hauntingly similar to the Babylonian account of creation that ancient Israel had so strongly opposed. In the Babylonian accounts, we see their "god of light"—named Marduk—splitting a dragon's body, and out of this split dragon, creating heaven and earth. Out of the dragon's blood, Marduk created human beings.[11] Like Hobbes, the Babylonians envision human beings as sinister at their core. And like Hobbes, the Babylonians believed that only a sovereign king could discipline and restrain these evil tendencies in the heart of humanity. For the Babylonians, it was the king of Babylon, as Marduk's representative on earth. For Hobbes, it was Leviathan. However, ancient Israel offered a contrasting vision of creation not as sinister at its core, but as "very good." Israel had learned, especially through exile and suffering, that God held the whole world in his hands because it had its origin in him, and had its true end in his eternal reason and love. It is difficult to look upon Hobbes's account of creation charitably. It not only seems to offer a bizarre inversion of the way communion works in Christ's Body; it also seems to be a strange repetition of an ancient pagan myth that takes a rather dim view of humanity, and a strong view of the state's power to protect us from what is sinister in us. Are modern political arrangements wedded to this understanding of creation? Is the formation of the nation-state wedded to the idea of Leviathan? What had occurred in theology to make such a transformation possible? As we consider the new relationship between Christianity and politics emerging in the modern period, these are questions we should keep before us.

In this chapter we have made a shift from the medieval relation between Christianity and politics to a distinctively modern relationship. Ferdinand and Isabella in the fifteenth

11. Benedict XVI, *In the Beginning*, 1–18.

century and Hobbes in the seventeenth century are book-ends for a massive historical shift that occurred in the space between them. As one mid-twentieth-century observer put it, the shift might be summed up this way: "If anybody in Europe is asked now who or what he is, his response is almost certain to be: 'I'm English,' or 'I'm Irish,'... or some other national. If a medieval European had been asked the question, he probably would have answered: 'I'm a Christian.'"[12] What has occurred in this shift is a fundamental change in how we imagine human identity and allegiance.

Charles Taylor has detailed how the conditions for belief changed from medieval European theistic cultures, in which it was nearly impossible not to believe in God, to modern national cultures in which faith in God was difficult.[13] In a similar fashion, Michael Allen Gillespie has argued that these shifts were due to earlier theological disputes in the medieval schools between realists and nominalists, or between those who believed in universal, transcendent truths and those who were convinced that truth is much more constrained and particular than this. What is clear from both Taylor's and Gillespie's accounts is that shifts in the understanding of God had occurred, and these theological shifts eventually changed how we imagine the human person and human community.[14] The image of Hobbes's *Leviathan* gives us a somewhat terrifying image of a mortal god. How did he arrive at a theology so different from the earlier Christian understanding of the triune God who has called humanity to communion with himself?

12. Hayes, *Nationalism*, 29.

13. See Taylor, *Secular Age*.

14. Gillespie, *Theological Origins of Modernity*.

In the second half of this book, we will examine how Christianity and politics learned new forms of relating to one another in the modern period. Having suggested that the sixteenth century is the crucial one for understanding the modern nature of the relationship between Christianity and politics, the next two chapters will pay special attention to theologians Martin Luther and John Calvin, as well as political theorists Niccolo Machiavelli, Thomas Hobbes, and John Locke, for it is the sixteenth century that so dramatically illustrates the shift from the medieval theology of participation in Christ's Body, to the modern, individualistic account of entering into the "social contract" of the "Hobbesian body politic."

SUGGESTED READING

Cavanaugh, William T. *The Myth of Religious Violence: Secular Ideology and the Roots of Modern Conflict.* Oxford: Oxford University Press, 2009.

Marx, Anthony. *Faith in Nation: Exclusionary Origins of Nationalism.* Oxford: Oxford University Press, 2005.

Gillespie, Michael Allen. *The Theological Origins of Modernity.* Chicago: University of Chicago Press, 2009.

SIX

Luther and Machiavelli

In his classic study on early modern political shifts, John Neville Figgis wrote that "it was the function of Luther ... to transfer to the State most of the prerogatives that had belonged in the Middle Ages to the Church."[1] Where the medieval mind with its complex distinctions could imagine many different parts gathered together into an organic social whole, the early modern mind was stressing discontinuities, dissolving the connective ligaments that held society together. It was becoming a world in which a thinker like Machiavelli could say that he loved the state more than his own soul, a world that could suddenly imagine itself becoming "unhinged" from the City of God. Yet according to Figgis, "the *Civitas Dei* of the Middle Ages received its death-blow from Luther."[2]

1. Figgis, *Political Thought*, 71.
2. Ibid., 77.

MARTIN LUTHER (1483–1546)

Martin Luther was an Augustinian monk, a Catholic
theologian with a reformist spirit. There were others who
preceded him in his attempts at church reform, but none
had received as much attention. Even if the ground of the
Protestant Reformation had been well-laid before Luther,
even if we recognize that Luther's legacy ultimately falls
prey to so many unintended consequences, and even if we
can be more sympathetic than Figgis in our estimation of
the reformer, Figgis is not wrong to credit Luther for ignit-
ing the fires of ecclesial division in the sixteenth century,
and in so doing, for changing the way we think about the
relationship between Christianity and politics.

A purist at heart, Luther desired a return to what he
imagined the early church to be: free of scholasticism's
speculative doctrine, free of philosophy, free of ecclesiastical authority and hierarchy, free of complexity, and most
importantly of all, free from the corruptions of politics. The
desire to distinguish the church from the political order
was Augustinian; but rather than the complex, commingled
view of Augustine's "two cities," Luther sought a purified
church that was free to be pure because the state was so
strong. It was a strange blend of positions that Augustine
would surely have been both for and against. In many ways,
Luther's was a utopian vision. However, it cannot be said
that Luther was politically naïve. In fact, the German reformer had a surprisingly high estimate of his own political
knowledge, writing of himself that "no one had taught, no
one had heard, and no one knew anything" more than he
"about temporal government, whence it came, what its office

and work was, or how it ought to serve God."[3] Considering the long preceding history of Christian political theology, such claims struck his contemporaries as less than modest. But how should it strike us? Even in his desire to purify the church of politics, Luther's project was politically ambitious. This ambition is worth closer inspection, and its impact on subsequent political theology should give us pause.

The most politically ambitious of all was Luther's attack on the papacy. After five hundred years of Protestant critiques of the papacy, Luther's protest against the Roman pontiff as a "foreign power," an affront to both the church and the state, is perhaps a tad boring. Yet we must remember that monarchs had been trying to counter the power of the papacy for centuries through methods as sinister as political assassination, anti-popes, and the threat of imperial armies. The investiture controversy, examined in chapter 4, was a prime example of this struggle between earthly and papal power early in its medieval ascent. Thus did Luther's protest converge with a long line of such political machinations.

Luther mobilized the masses, especially in lands where the ruling elites were sympathetic to any cause that could draw the Catholic masses into new forms of allegiance. And with the princes that supported the Reformation, Luther challenged medieval conceptions of the papacy. But Luther did not wish to divide the church, or to demolish the papacy, only to "reform" it. However, as his reforms met resistance from the very juridical structures of the church's hierarchy that he sought to reform, he came to believe that the only path to spiritual reform and renewal would be to reject the institutional structures themselves, if only for a time. He

3. Luther, *Luther's Works*, 5:81.

saw the papacy and council in merely "external" political-juridical terms, and thus believed that the church could be itself without these "externalities"; indeed, Luther thought his rejection of them might reveal a more authentically Christian church. Thus did Luther seek a genuine good: the revitalization of the spiritual life of the church. However, his mode of achieving this was genuinely destructive—he believed reformation would require that the majority of the medieval external structures, the hierarchy, the sacramental system, the penitential system, would all have to be brought down in favor of a more internalized, spiritualized, and "democratized" form of the Christian life. The theological instrument used for this demolition was "the priesthood of all believers."

The phrase "priesthood of all believers" is derived from the New Testament epistle attributed to the Apostle Peter: "you are a chosen race, a royal priesthood, a holy nation" (1 Pet 2:9). In the context of the epistle, the church itself is called to be "built into a spiritual house, to be a holy priesthood, to offer spiritual sacrifices acceptable to God through Jesus Christ" (1 Pet 2:5). The Catholic tradition interpreted being a holy priesthood as liturgical participation in the body of Christ, who, in the words of the epistle to the Hebrews, is the one true mediator and high priest (Heb 9–10). Thus Catholics held that the only spiritual sacrifice to be offered was the sacrifice that Christ himself had made, and certain Christians were ordained as priests to celebrate this gift of grace in the Eucharistic feast. Participation in the Eucharist was participation in this holy priesthood for all. The Petrine epistle uses first personal plural language; it is profoundly communal. Luther, on the other hand, unwittingly made the text work in a much more individualistic way, shifting the priesthood from a corporate, participatory identity to a highly reductive view of all individual believers as priests making their own private spiritual sacrifices to God through Jesus Christ.[4] Luther's reading of 1 Peter did not make perfect sense of the epistle, but his interpretation of this text in terms of "the priesthood of all believers" provided powerful support for his political claim that the hierarchy of deacons, priests, and bishops ran counter to the gospel.

As we have noted, Luther wanted to revitalize the spiritual life of the church and thought that in order to do so, he must also "depoliticize" it. "The priesthood of all believers" and his increasing alliance with "temporal authority" (which he also derives in part from his reading of 1 Peter) help him achieve this "spiritual renewal." When the juridical, institutional nature of the ecclesial hierarchy had been "depoliticized," and any power the church had was internalized or "spiritualized" in the faith of individuals, the church nevertheless still required a concrete, visible structure that would enable it to flourish. However, denying the ecclesial any significant political structure, Luther transferred it instead to the state, effectively granting the "temporal authority" a monopoly on power. For fifteen hundred years the church itself had been a counter-weight to temporal authority in the church. Yet because of Luther's desire for purity, and his view that politics could only be negative—as a consequence of the Fall—his reforms effectively handed

4. For a more sympathetic, ecumenically hopeful, yet selective account of Luther in continuity with both Eastern and Western aspects of the Catholic tradition of communal, participatory deification, see Braaten and Jenson, eds., *Union with Christ*.

all power to emerging national authorities—the early modern nation-states.

Since Luther viewed the institutional side of church
life as an obstacle to authentic faith, he was eager to give as
much of the institutional power of the church as possible to
the state. As Sheldon Wolin puts it, "The institutional weakness of the Church made it no match for the secular power
that Luther had rationalized. The end-product was the ter-
ritorial Church (*Landeskirche*)."[5] It is ironic that a thinker
who was so opposed to the political nature of the church
gave birth to the state-church in Germany; but once Luther
had made "authentic faith" dependent only upon the spiritual, eschewing the mediating structures of the sacramental
economy of the church, then everything external about the
church could only be supported by some other authority.
In Wolin's quite critical estimation, Luther drove a wedge
between the church and state, only to make the church
dependent upon the state. He appears as an Augustinian
whose political theology achieves the very opposite of
Augustine's.

From an Augustinian point of view—already hinted
at above in our alternative account of the priesthood of all
believers—a crucial problem with Luther's view of grace is
his conviction that it is always unmediated, interior, and
invisible. This was a significant departure from a tradition
of thinking about the grace of God as necessarily mediated
through Christ's body, in the one, holy, catholic church. As
an Augustinian monk, part of Luther's formation was in
reading works by Saint Augustine. Augustine had always
been associated with the view that human nature was fallen

5. Wolin, *Politics and Vision,* 133

and therefore incapable of being virtuous except through the grace of God given in the body of Christ. Some earlier medieval theologians had also associated Augustine with the view that human government was a consequence of the Fall, and that human government was thus a kind of "necessary evil," allowed by God in order "to punish the wicked and to praise the righteous" (according to 1 Pet 2:14). Luther's habit was to pick up such Augustinian themes, often in isolation from other complicating themes, and then radicalize them to profoundly different effect.

Moreover, Luther's insistence on "Scripture alone" and "faith alone" also individualized the way the Bible and faith had been understood in the Christian community— quite in keeping with the nominalist emphasis upon the individual will that had been stressed in the preceding two centuries. Rather than viewing the church as Christ's body on pilgrimage through time, guided by the Holy Spirit in its holy task of understanding the faith that it had been given through the Scriptures, through the tradition of the Fathers and Councils of the church, Luther's theological claims suggested that a dramatic break from this history was necessary for the church to be pure and authentic.

For Luther, the church as *institution* with laws, canons, dogmas, rules, rituals—external structures and practices— was a church that needed to be reformed and spiritually reawakened. In the context of a Catholic Church that had overemphasized the juridical and legal dimensions of the church, we can perhaps sympathize with Luther's desire to recover a more spiritual and mystical view of the church. We might recall how Bernard of Clairvaux had raised similar concerns during the investiture controversy. Yet we must also recognize that however good his intentions, Luther's theological interventions contributed to a process of transferring power from church to state. By insisting on an "interiorized" and "spiritualized" church, Luther made a church so institutionally weak that it *needed* the state. However, to be fair, he also laid the foundations for thinking about how the state needed "the priesthood of all believers."

Luther's teaching on "the priesthood of all believers" was an attempt to rethink the ordered distinctions between lay and religious vocations, and thus to minimize the importance of the hierarchical structures of the medieval church. On one level we can see in Luther's thought the origins of a radically democratic view of the church. But his idealized, individualized, and interiorized ecclesiology also served to accentuate a wedge between the individual and the community that was emerging at the time. It retrospect we can see how Luther's teaching places a justificatory spiritual veil over his own individual political break from the authority of the Catholic Church. Most importantly, as we have seen, by depoliticizing the church he necessarily substantializes the state; Luther provides the emerging nation-states with a theological *raison d'etre* that they might not otherwise have had. In Luther's vision, the state now serves as the visible provision necessary for the church to exist in a sinful world. He writes:

> There are few true believers, and still fewer who live a Christian life, who do not resist evil and indeed themselves do no evil. For this reason God has provided for them a different government beyond the Christian estate and kingdom of God. He has subjected them to the sword so that,

> even though they would like to, they are unable to
> practice their wickedness, and if they do practice
> it they cannot do so without fear or with success
> and impunity.[6]

While Luther is quick to underline that true believers have no need of either the sword or the law, he is doubly quick to say that the world is not full of true believers, and until it is so, both the sword and the law are necessary. His approach is to insist that the church cannot rule the world in "a Christian and evangelical manner" and thus "the masses" *must be ruled by some other body*—a temporal authority— the state. Luther is emphatic: "It is out of the question that there should be a common Christian government over the whole world." As a result, the "two governments" must be carefully distinguished from each other, since one promotes "righteousness" and the other prevents evil deeds. In simple terms, the church has a positive function, and the state has a negative one.

This puts the "true believer" in an interesting position with regard to "two governments." For while the Christian with a liberated conscience has no need of the law or sword of state, Luther believes that out of love of neighbor the Christian is "under obligation to serve and assist the sword by whatever means,"[7] because without temporal laws, the wicked would be unrestrained and allowed to wreak havoc with the gentle. Not only out of Christian love ought temporal governments be obeyed, but also out of fear, for without temporal authority the "wolves would devour the sheep." Luther explains: "For this reason God has ordained two

6. Luther, "Temporal Authority," in *Luther's Works*, 45:90.
7. Ibid., 45:95.

governments: the spiritual, by which the Holy Spirit pro-
duces Christians and righteous people under Christ; and
the temporal, which restrains the un-Christian and wicked
so that—no thanks to them—they are obliged to keep still
and maintain an outward peace."[8] Furthermore, "that the
essential governmental authority may not be despised and
become enfeebled or perish . . . [t]he world cannot and dare
not dispense with it."[9]

On the one hand, Luther wants Christians to have
nothing to do with temporal affairs, and thus entirely spiri-
tualizes the church. On the other hand, he wants Christians
to do everything in their power to strengthen and support
the state, and he thus makes the church a servant of the state.
It is a troubling political paradox that deepens rather than
solves the Augustinian problematic. Rather than placing the
church above the state, Luther actually encourages the view
that church and state are not only mutually beneficial, but
mutually necessary given the sinful state of human nature.
Given Luther's separatist streak, it is ironically a view that
Emperor Constantine could have shared.

Once Luther finally broke with the pope and the council, and replaced these entirely with "the priesthood of all
believers," his revolutionary understanding of the church
would come to its full political effect, for then the church
would outwardly depend upon secular rulers for its safety,
but inwardly rely upon Christ alone. In Wolin's view, by
handing over all political power to the secular rulers and
wresting it all away from the church, Luther effectively
gave the temporal rulers a monopoly on all kinds of power.

8. Ibid., 45:91.
9. Ibid., 45:95.

Likewise, Figgis observes, "By the destruction of the inde-
pendence of the Church and its hold on an extra-territorial
public opinion, the last obstacle to the unity of the State was
removed."[10] Yet we should also consider John Bossy's com-
ment on how so much of this was beyond Luther's intention
or control. Bossy writes,

> A sense of fatality, of results achieved which were
> the opposite of those intended, hangs over their
> efforts: as if the current of social and cultural
> evolution which was carrying them forward was
> at the same time pushing them aside into shallow
> waters. In the Lutheran case the ambition to re-
> store a communal eucharist resulted in a practice
> of communion as individualist and asocial as that
> of the Counter-Reformation.[11]

While Figgis and Wolin are not so sympathetic to Luther,
history shows Luther falling prey to unintended consequences. His political vision seemed, in a certain sense,
beyond control.

What begins to emerge is that the sixteenth-century
transfer of power had two sides to it: on the one side, Luther
depoliticized religion; and on the other, Machiavelli and
other Italian humanists worked hard to *detheologize politics*. Importantly for our argument, both sides enabled the
rise of early nation-states. Wolin has argued that Luther can
best be understood through his basic urge towards simpli-
fication (his "simplistic imperative" being akin to Occam's
nominalist razor)—towards a more primitive purity against
the political complexities of ecclesial hierarchies and the

10. Figgis, *Political Thought*, 72.
11. Bossy, "Mass as a Social Institution," 29–61.

theological complexities of scholasticism. Luther sought to forge a new religious vocabulary wiped clean of these medieval accretions and freed of all political detritus. Though in this very simplistic imperative, yet another paradox arose: his depoliticized religious thought exercised a profound influence on the later evolution of political ideas. Luther's church became so institutionally weak that it could only be sustained by a secular power that he had rationalized through his theology.

Just as medieval court lawyers had denied ecclesiastical power through spiritualizing the power of state (in the divine right of kings), so Luther denied ecclesiastical power by entirely spiritualizing the power of the church. The sixteenth century brings to an end the medieval view that "the State is but a department of the Church" and re-asserts the autonomy of the state. The power of the prince is not mediated by any ecclesiastical authority; authority comes from God through the individual consciences of the people. Luther plays a role in helping to give the state the power to form the conscience, the power to collect mass allegiances, the power to form a people. The state is now unhinged from any other institutional authority that could morally check its power; the state is free to construct itself, and conduct itself, according to its own norms. Thus did Martin Luther set the stage for Niccolò Machiavelli's dramatic entry.

NICCOLÒ MACHIAVELLI (1469–1527)

Niccolò Machiavelli was from the city of Florence and had political duties in that republican city-state before it fell in 1512,[12] when the Medicis took over and Machiavelli was imprisoned, tortured, and then effectively exiled from 1513–1527. It is interesting to consider that both Luther and Machiavelli transformed Western political thought each in different states of banishment. Machiavelli wrote *The Prince* in 1513, his *Discourses* in 1517, and his *Art of War* in 1520—all during his exile from Florentine politics, perhaps all written with the hope of being employed in politics once again. Luther posted his famous ninety-five theses at the University of Wittenberg in October of 1517, and by 1520 he had been excommunicated by the Catholic Church. Both men were insiders that became outsiders, exiles from their original homelands (Florence and the Catholic Church). Both men engaged in acts of deconstruction and reconstruction of the social and political frameworks from which they came. Moreover, both thinkers wanted different kinds of separation and autonomy. In search of reform, Luther unhinged the church from its visible, juridical, institutional structures, giving it a kind of spiritual autonomy. In search of autonomy, Machiavelli unhinged politics from its relationship to the church's theology and ethical absolutes. In addition, Luther wanted a radical break from a highly developed tradition of hierarchy, and Machiavelli sought to upend the aristocratic and Medicean view of patronage politics that he believed weakened republican institutions. Both men achieved their own kinds of success: Luther founded a reform movement, and Machiavelli gave voice to the rise of the modern state.

12. Machiavelli had been, for fourteen years, the secretary of a high-level committee charged with advising the government on military and foreign affairs.

How did Machiavelli do it? Wolin argues that there are at least four important points in Machiavelli's thought that enable him to construct a new political idea, meaning a new kind of "principality" and a new kind of "prince."[13] Machiavelli (1) redefines virtue in terms of the state; (2) redefines violence and coercion as virtues in service of the state; (3) redefines politics as the management of interest-conflict; and (4) creates a new mythology of the nation built on the idea of the *corpus mysticum*. In each of these four points, we can see that Machiavelli is the political theorist that enshrines the superiority of the state over all other concerns.

1. Redefine Virtue

Machiavelli is so often associated with being deceptive that we could be forgiven for thinking that he completely detaches politics from any classical or Christian conception of the Good or the True.

We commonly think of Machiavelli as "unethical," thus the adjective "Machiavellian" to describe a politics of deception. There is some truth to this as Machiavelli did advocate practical expediency and cunning, where deceitful means could be justified by ends which served the needs of the state (a true father of utilitarian ethics). However, it is not true that he rejected entirely the application of virtues in politics. Rather, Machiavelli radically changed the nature of those virtues and the standard for judging what counted as virtue. He argued that it was not nature, or God, the society or the church which determined what counted as virtue,

13. See Wolin, *Politics and Vision*, 175–213.

rather it was the needs of the state that set the ethical standard. If Machiavelli loved his country more than his own
soul (as he proudly claimed), we can see that for him the
state replaced the church. A shift in virtues was thus inevitable. What interested him most was the kind of knowledge,
standards, and virtues that were relevant to the new, modern politics that were aimed at the well being and perpetuity of the state, not of the church. Machiavelli did not detach
politics and virtue, he redefined virtue politically.

Crucial to his account of the virtues was the break he
made with prior accounts of political virtue that, under the
influence of the church's doctrine of creation, privileged the
common good discernible by the conscience, the law written by God on every human heart. This common good was
transcendent, eternal, and divine; political virtue consisted
in discerning this common good from a conscience well
formed in communion with Christ. Machiavelli was able
to upset this view of political virtue, seeking to eclipse the
conception of natural law entirely (for natural law was itself
a limit on politics).[14] He argued for the external character
of political knowledge, suggesting that politics had more
to do with mechanisms and techniques for control of the
populace than with the virtues internal to political actors.
He thus exteriorized virtue in a way that stressed the appearance of public virtues, whether they were there or not.
So a modern politician could appear to have the virtue of
honesty, but lie to protect his office, the lie being justified as
a means to protect his tenure in a powerful political office,
an end that could be claimed for the greater good. The state,
once again, had become an end in itself.

14. Figgis, *Political Thought,* 97.

2. Redefine the Relation between Violence and the State

In another sense, Machiavelli redefined virtue as *virtù*, or those "masculine" characteristics of force necessary to secure the state, to maintain the state, and to achieve "greatness and glory" for the state. The state exists through coercive authority over a set territory, and thus violence is always justified whenever it serves the ends of the state. Thus the state would necessarily require a standing army, and the military, in turn, would be the model for civic virtue because the military secures the highest good, which is the state itself.

It is easy to miss the point that violence is now *justified* in a way that it had not been during the medieval period, but there is more than this; Machiavelli's redefinition of virtue and his redeployment of virtue in relation to the state makes war a natural condition for the strong state that is seeking greatness and glory. Thus does Machiavelli advise the prince that his citizenry should be kept poor and concerned only about the security of possessions; and to this end, Machiavelli thinks it is *best for the state* to be continually at war; such a condition would help to generate the continual growth of the state.

3. Redefine Politics as Institutional Interest-Cconflict Management

If politics is no longer about a common good, and it is instead about the stability and strength of the state, then there arises a need to carefully manage any interests among the people that could potentially conflict with the interests of the state. Machiavelli recognized the need for institutions that could facilitate and shape the conflicts of interest in a relatively stable manner.

Machiavelli argued that if you had the right laws and the right institutions, the people would have the virtues of those external instruments *impressed upon them*, and that this would in turn support the institutions. It was a formula for political survival. After the founding prince died ("the King is dead, long live the King"), the political order or "state" he founded could survive through those institutions that managed the vicissitudes of the peoples' conflicting interests. Machiavelli had found a formula for alleviating the dependence of the state on hereditary princes, for in his view the hereditary principle was a very weak one in the establishment of a strong state. Instead, the strength of the state is secured by institutions that maintain the administrative structure after the death of the prince—in a sense, the mystical body of the old medieval view of the King's two bodies had now been officially transferred to the state. If politics could be dealt with systematically through institutions, then the state would theoretically be able to survive in perpetuity, much as the Catholic Church had done for 1500 years.

4. Create a New Mythology of Nation to Secure Unity

The language of the church had to be recast to accord with the nationalization of religious life. Machiavelli saw that an alliance was forming between those who were advocating the reform of the church (such as Luther) and those who were concerned to create nation-states that were autonomous and independent of the church. Thus it was not simply enough to define virtue for the ends of the state; the state also needed a mythology that could provide some other basis for unity than the church. In this we must keep in mind that one of Machiavelli's driving concerns was the unity of Italy. It is often said that he was an "objective realist," the founder of *realpolitik,* but a close look at the closing chapters of *The Prince* reveals him as a passionate nationalist intent on reframing the state as a new kind of *corpus mysticum.* He was not afraid to employ the language of the church on his crusade to unify Italy.

Consider the metaphors he uses for Italy. Towards the end of *The Prince,* he exhorts the readers to free Italy from "the barbarians" in terms oddly reminiscent of Augustine's *The City of God Against the Pagans.* He writes, "if, as I said, it was necessary for the people of Israel to be enslaved in Egypt to make known the virtue of Moses . . . then at present, to make known the virtue of an Italian spirit, it was necessary for Italy to be reduced to her present conditions, and that she be more enslaved than the Hebrews."[15] Long before America was likened to Israel, to Jerusalem, the original city on a hill, Machiavelli likened Italy to "the promised land of greatness and glory."

Machiavelli first compares Italy to the ancient Israelites who were redeemed from bondage under the Egyptians and became a nation with a Redeemer, namely God acting through Moses. For the church, Israel's Redeemer had personally come to save humanity, being made man in Jesus Christ. Yet for Machiavelli, a new redeemer is expected. He imagines Italy "left as lifeless" and awaiting "the man who may heal her wounds . . . who can cure her of those sores

15. Machiavelli, *The Prince,* 87.

that have been festering for so long."[16] It is as if Italy is the body of Christ who had suffered and died on the Cross, now being buried and "left as lifeless," awaiting resurrection. This is precisely what Machiavelli looks forward to: the resurrection of Italy as a new *corpus Christi*, perhaps even a new *corpus mysticum*.

"Everything," Machiavelli writes of Italy, "has converged for your greatness." The image he paints is of biblical proportion, drawing on the book of Exodus most explicitly: "we now see here extraordinary, unprecedented signs brought about by God: the sea has opened up; a cloud has shown you the path; the rock has poured forth; here manna has rained."[17] Just as he likens Italy to the body of Christ, he also likens Italy to Israel. Indeed, in terms very much reminiscent of how the church speaks of itself as the new Israel, Machiavelli generates myth for the sake of nation, and inserts the state in place of the redeeming body that was once the church. In his distorted view, both God and the church looked favorably on this shift, and he saw a sign of support for this in the fact that a Florentine politician, Giovanni de Medici, had recently become Pope Leo X (the very same pope who excommunicated Luther in 1521).

Tellingly, Machiavelli's "new Israel" is not redeemed by grace, but by glory: "everything converging for your greatness." He always refers to Italy in an almost church-like way as "Your Illustrious House." And he exhorts his Italian princes, "God does not wish to do everything." God has only led them to the promised land: "the rest you must

16. Ibid., 88.
17. Ibid.

do for yourself."[18] Italy could only be redeemed and unified by prudence, political wit, and force; creating a certain mythology was an essential part of that need to reconstitute the allegiances of the people around a new body politic. Comparing Italy to both Israel and the body of Christ gave power to a new identity being formed around nation.

It was only by creating a new mythology that a prince could capture the imaginations of the people, the Italian nation, to draw their allegiances to the emerging state—"to surprise and captivate" them with the idea of a nation-state. Only this would justify their sacrifices when conflicts of interest inevitably would arise. It was a formula for preferring national identity and unity to any other kind of unified identity (e.g., ecclesial identity and unity). Machiavelli could even justify his modern political ethics by way of the biblical narrative. After all, Moses himself used cruelty and lies in order to save Israel and remained God's friend. Indeed, he would argue, God was a friend of states and used new political orders for the redemption of people. *True religion*, for Machiavelli, was only *the religion of state*.

Machiavelli was more than an "objective realist," the founder of "political science"; he was also a passionate nationalist who championed the view that the state was an end in itself, and that the unity of the nation was all that mattered; Italy above all else. Italy itself was the new *corpus Christi*; and the prince, *with the support of the masses*, was to work heroically for political redemption purely in national terms. Machiavelli's thought emerged just as monarchs had begun to centralize their powers around new ideas: an emerging sense of a national consciousness was pushing

18. Ibid.

towards an autonomous political order across Europe, and towards America, insisting that Christian norms be at the service of national interest. Quietly, a number of forces had combined to shift mass allegiances.

As Sheldon Wolin writes, "nationalism and patriotism had not yet reached a position of being able to furnish from their own resources a code of civic conduct independent of religion," but the reformation process, which Luther helped to consolidate, would help to dissolve religious authority and likewise help to establish a new unity through national feeling and loyalty.[19] What nationalistic fervor enabled was *a predictable source of mass consent.* Machiavelli realized that the energies of the masses were far more powerful than monarchs, including bishops and popes, and that political orders had lost touch with this untapped power of the people. The people would be a new *corpus mysticum* to which the state would need to regularly return for renewal and revivification.[20] Then the state would also be in a position to shape the masses, to form the people in the virtues necessary for sustaining itself.

Machiavelli had changed the source, purpose, and the whole scale of virtues to serve the state—much as they had served the state in classical republics—and he aided in a process that would ensure that mass allegiance could shift from one *corpus Christi* to another. The hope was that Luther's spiritualized church would fade from sight as the state came into clear, concrete focus. That hope seemed to come from both Machiavelli and Luther, though in different ways. In the view of J. N. Figgis, "the invisibility of the

19. Wolin, *Politics and Vision*, 177.
20. Ibid., 184.

Church is, in fact, to Luther the condition and the counterpart of the visibility of the State—which in its full sense is a new thing."[21] Machiavelli, with Luther's unwitting and unintended assistance, helped change "the admiration of men from the saintly to the civic virtues," and both men helped to transfer the "halo of sanctity that had hitherto been mainly the privilege of the ecclesiastical" to "the holiness of the State."[22]

SUGGESTED READINGS

Martin Luther, *Luther: Selected Political Writings* (Eugene, OR: Wipf & Stock, 2003).

Niccolò Machiavelli, *The Prince* (Oxford: Oxford University Press, 2008).

John Neville Figgis, *Political Thought from Gerson to Grotius: 1414–1625* (New York: Harper, 1960).

David Steinmetz, *Luther in Context* (Grand Rapids: Baker, 2002).

21. Figgis, *Political Thought*, 88.
22. Ibid., 93.

SEVEN

Between Calvin and Hobbes

John Calvin corrects the anti-institutional and potentially individualistic implications of Luther's ecclesiology, recovering for the Reformation what the Catholic Church had always known: a religious society, like any other society, must find support in institutions, and that institutions, in turn, are aggregates of power.[1] The recovery, however, could not mean reconciliation of ecclesial divisions. In this chapter we examine historical events that gave rise to a new relationship between Christianity and politics, between the sixteenth-century Reformation and the eighteenth-century founding of modern democracies such as France, England, and America, and in a certain way, between Calvin and Hobbes.

JOHN CALVIN (1509–1564)

For John Calvin, Luther's arrangement was too simplistic with regard to institutions, too individualistic with regard

1. Wolin, *Politics and Vision*, 153.

to faith, and too pessimistic with regard to the state. A lawyer by training, Calvin saw the law in much more positive terms than Luther did, and thus did not see the state as purely debased. As a result he did not try to drive a wedge between church and state, and his positive regard for the institutional structures of the church meant that he did not make a spiritualized church dependent on a substantialized state.

Partly in reaction to Luther, Calvin was trying to restore the reputation of the political order, and like Catholic theologians before him, he was trying to build bridges between Christian virtues and the civic virtues of the state and society. The term he sometimes used was "common grace," though much of the thinking amounted to a return to the Christian preference for "natural law" that had predominated in the medieval period. The great contribution of the Geneva theologian was that he understood that an invisible, mystical unity was not enough, and that visible unity must find support in institutions, offices, doctrines, laws, and ritual action. Calvin saw that Luther's liberation of the individual conscience from external hierarchical or historical authorities overlooked a fundamental need: *a conscience needed a community*. Calvin understood that conscience was formed and nurtured in families and societies that are themselves formed, maintained, and nurtured by social and political institutions. The common good of all depended on the cultivation of the conscience. His answer to Luther's individual conscience was the communal conscience. Calvin's collective conscience was one formed by the church, but also by civil society and civil government. The conscience is disciplined and trained in those virtues that participate in the good that is common to all. Indeed, the good that is common to all is God. It is not surprising, then, that for a time Calvin himself favored a theocracy, a complex ordering of church, state, and civil society in which God is central to each sphere. In certain respects, Calvin is making up for Luther's excesses. He brings back complexity in the wake of Luther's simplistic imperative.

The value of political unity (across these spheres) especially returns to the fore as Calvin began to absorb political vocabulary back into the liturgical life of the church. While Luther had tried to strip the church's liturgical language of all its political significance, Calvin stressed the priority of the church in forming a politically virtuous people. He believed that good Christians make good citizens and, importantly, he also believed that to be a good citizen is at least halfway to being a good Christian (for any good in one sphere must be at least partially good in every sphere if the good is genuinely common). Thus the relationship between Christianity and politics—the politics of state and civil society—is a complementary one for Calvin. He is not utopian about this, especially after the failures of his theocratic experiments in Geneva, but he does see that a complex intermingling of relations between church, state, and society is not only possible, but a necessary corollary of belief in the common good. In a strange recrudescent twist, Calvin's view is much closer to the medieval framework, and yet the damage of ecclesial division had been done, and thus his semi-"return" to a medieval political theology could not turn back the clock.

What is so interesting about Calvin's renovation work is that the shift he makes from individual conscience to collective or communal conscience meant that he had, in fact, returned to the idea of *participation*, or "incorporation into the body of Christ."[2] However, once again this participation was no longer focused on what it had meant to participate in the Body of Christ through the Eucharist in the Catholic sacramental framework. Ever the reformer, Calvin saw participation in terms of participating in the preaching of the Gospel as the good that is common to all. That made preaching central as well as political education in society. For Calvin, participation in the institutions of state and civil society were also spheres in which God was sovereign, and thus, since all authority was ordained by the Word of God, participation in the state and civil society could be understood as profoundly compatible. Calvin sought to recover a society that could be at once well ordered, disciplined, and cohesive, but *without any visible head* (i.e., without a pope). The Word of God alone could be authoritative, making the preaching of the Word of God absolutely central, moving the sermon, rather than the Eucharist, to the center of worship.

In sum, Calvin saw the Word of God as the source of authority not only for the church, but also for state and society. All persons of authority were ministers of this Word. Politicians in Europe are often called "ministers of state" precisely because of a Calvinistic preference for seeing state office-holders as parallel to ministers of God's Word, only in a different sphere.[3] The unity, the cohesion

2. John Calvin, *Institutes of the Christian Religion* III.11.10.

3. Thomas Hobbes will incorporate this aspect of Calvin's theology, making it serve his political philosophy, "seeing then in every Christian commonwealth, the civil sovereign is the supreme pastor

of the society, would not be held together by a Pope, or an Emperor, or even by the Eucharist—the unity and cohesion that Calvin sought were a complex unity dependent upon mass participation in a political and social order that was part of the divine order of God's Word. If Luther's theology had made Christians more dependent upon the visibility of state structures, then Calvin's theology served to cata-lyze Christian masses for social action, and as the primary shapers of institutions of state and economy for the sake of the common good.[4] For Calvin, the Christian life and the civic life alike were morally strenuous endeavors in a life directed to the greater glory of God.

Calvin differed greatly from Luther's much-maligned (and misunderstood) advice to Philipp Melanchthon to "sin boldly." Unlike Luther, Calvin stressed "sanctification by works." This contrast is crucial for understanding Calvin's treatment of conscience, for it contributes to the idea of the *corpus mysticum* being transferred to the state, the econo-my, and the civil society. Originally, in the medieval frame, conscience involved the *intellectual* awareness of guilt (as in a "bad conscience"). Because of sin, the conscience was not free; rather, the conscience needed to be educated, formed in the truth, and this formation was a crucial to the discernment of virtues and vices. The conscience was formed in a complex moral grammar within a penitential culture ordered to the city of God. However, for Luther, the conscience was an "inwardness of spirit," a "feeling for

---

. . . from the civil sovereign…all other pastors derive their right of teaching, preaching, and other functions . . . they are but *his* ministers" (*Leviathan*, 361).

4. See Max Weber's famous account of Calvin's social, political, and economic views in *Protestant Ethic and the Spirit of Capitalism*.

the divine" that was itself a resource for the individual to identify, within the pious soul, the sinful nature of our actions, and thus to drive us always further into a state of dependence upon God for grace. Luther's promulgation of the individual, "liberated" conscience was a direct attack on the authoritative structures of a hierarchical communion, but Calvin saw the corrosive implications of this for the church. It is not unreasonable, then, to see Calvin's "collective conscience" as an ecclesiological correction of Luther's stress on the individual conscience.[5]

Sheldon Wolin has understood the political implications of these shifts from the individual to the communal conscience within the Reformation. He argues that with Hobbes, Calvin's "collective conscience" became the "social conscience." And he argues that with Locke, Hobbes's "social conscience" was reduced to the management of interest-conflicts and thus was reduced to "economic interest." Thus, according to Wolin, what really binds us together in the new "Hobbesian" body politic is not the conscience at all—it is the economy. The economy becomes the new common good. The economy is what is in the "public interest," for it is the economy that is the true maintainer of the state and the great arbiter of interest-conflict.

It is easy to see in retrospect how one reformulation of "conscience" could be used by Luther to detach human beings from one church culture, and how another reformulation could be used by Calvin to reattach human beings to another kind of church culture. Perhaps it is more difficult

5. See Wolin's subtle argument concerning the shifting role of the conscience in Luther, Calvin and Hobbes in *Politics and Vision*, 127–314.

to imagine the political implications. However, that process of detachment and reattachment, in which the conscience was a useful tool, mobilized mass sentiment for the formation of a new set of social and political relations, and a new set of selective and secular allegiances. It was inevitable that the relationship between Christianity and politics would change. Luther and Calvin, in different ways, and in certain respects quite unintentionally, aided this process. However, the most dramatic shifts were far beyond the control of either of these two Protestant theologians. The most dramatic shifts are best seen through the eyes of Thomas Hobbes and in the so-called "wars of religion" that he witnessed in his beloved England.

THOMAS HOBBES (1588–1679)

A couple generations after Calvin, the political philosopher Thomas Hobbes would also attempt a complex arrangement between church, society, and state, to a different effect, but one made possible by debates amongst the Reformers about how to re-imagine the relationship between Christianity and politics. The Hobbesian relationship between the masses and the state is different from Calvin's idea, not least because of their differing historical contexts. The civil wars that Hobbes observed were bloody and chaotic. At bottom, Hobbes lived in a world of fear. The "wars of religion" that he had observed gave rise to the thought that humans were not only, as Aristotle believed, political animals: they were also *violent animals*. Hobbes view of human nature was a caricature of the Calvinistic doctrine of the total depravity of man, prone to quarrel; as Hobbes put it, "every man, against every man."[6] Perhaps his view of human nature was just what he had observed about human life in his day: "solitary, poor, nasty, brutish, and short."[7] For Luther and Calvin alike, Jesus Christ, the Word of God incarnate, had saved humanity from sin. Hobbes was unconvinced. He believed in God and had a great deal of knowledge of the Bible, but he also thought the Catholic Church was idolatrous (most especially in its Eucharistic practice). He was far more comfortable talking about natural bodies rather than supernatural ones, and he was more comfortable with "civil worship" than he was with "divine worship," which he thought was so fraught with the risks of idolatry.

With bloodshed all around him, it is hardly surprising that Hobbes hoped for some "real and present" savior in a strong, sovereign political body which he calls Leviathan: "a common power to keep them all in awe."[8] If the mystical unity received by grace in the Eucharistic worship of God did not seem possible, a natural unity would be required. If unity could not be received as a divine gift in the Body of Christ, if it could not be established by God's will, it would have to be achieved through the work of conforming to the sovereign will of Leviathan, a "*Mortal God*" to be "our peace and defence [*sic*]."[9]

Hobbes, like Machiavelli, passionately, fervently, and actively imagines visionary portraits of political reality. He is far from objective and dispassionate, but like Machiavelli, in constructing a new political body through his imagina-

6. Hobbes, *Leviathan*, 84.
7. Ibid.
8. Ibid.
9. Ibid., 114. Emphasis mine.

tion, he also developed a technical and scientific language designed to make us forget that Leviathan is artificial. Hobbes wants his public to forget that the new rules of the republic are based on a fiction. He is well aware that his political theory is constructed *ex nihilo*. It is constructed to aid a society in its exchange of one political culture for another. Hobbes thought that a country torn apart by the anarchy of liberated individual consciences, ablaze with "inner lights," underlined the need for an overarching unity out of a diversity of private interests and private reasons. Like Calvin, Hobbes was trying to set things right after the break-up of the medieval arrangements. "All the king's horses and all the king's men" might not be able to put humpty dumpty back together again, but a new social unity could be constructed. Perhaps a new *corpus mysticum* could be made, as God made the world, out of nothing. However, this new *corpus mysticum* would be humanly constructed: we would create a mortal god to save us from ourselves. But what sort of god did Hobbes create, and why were the "wars of religion" so crucial?

WARS OF RELIGION

Catholic theologian William Cavanaugh has recently argued that we have not correctly understood the relationship between the wars of religion and the emergence of nation-state politics. The standard account has been that the Protestant Reformation was a catalyst for the wars of religion and that these wars between Catholics and Protestants threatened to tear Europe apart. The solution in the standard account was the creation of a liberal nation-state to protect us from our "brutish" human nature. America, on this account, was the crowning achievement of this triumph of the liberal state over the divisive power of religion.

Cavanaugh argues that this standard account actually has it backwards. The "wars of religion" did not necessitate "the birth of the modern state." On the contrary, the wars of religion "were in fact the birthpangs of the state."[10] Rather than think of the "wars of religion" being "about religion," they are really about the struggle to form the modern nation-state. The wars were not fought as a conflict between Catholicism and Protestantism—they were fought "over the decaying remnants of the medieval ecclesial order."[11] Elites of the emerging nation-states sought to capitalize on the privatization of religion (see chapter 6) and to make religion an instrument of "national interest" so that it could effectively secure for itself the temporal powers that hung in the balance after the crumbling of the medieval edifice. The wars of religion fought in the sixteenth and seventeenth centuries were wars sponsored by state elites in order "to invert the dominance of the ecclesiastical over the civil authorities."[12]

Even if Cavanaugh is only half right about state agency in the wars of religion, it must be said that state violence helped to complete the transfer of power that had been in process for centuries. Charles V used his military might as a Catholic ruler not to attack the Lutherans in Wittenberg, but to attack *papal powers* in Rome. When the Holy Roman Emperor turned his armies on Protestants in 1547—initiat-

10. Cavanaugh, *Theopolitical Imagination*, 22.
11. Ibid.
12. Ibid., 23.

ing the first of the Wars—it became clear that secular rulers, whether Catholic or Protestant, cared very little about doctrinal differences between Christians, but cared a great deal for how their political authority could be centralized and secured. Eight years later, that initial war resulted in the Peace of Augsburg, which declared that every prince could choose his own religion for his region: *cuius regio, eius religio*. It meant that religion could now be legally placed in the hands of the princes to be *used for the purposes of their states*. Machiavelli's prescriptions were prophetic. Catholic and Protestant princes could be seen to sponsor "true religion" at the same time as they used "religion" as means to an end.

One problem for Cavanaugh's argument might be put in the way of a question: *why have we forgotten this?* That is, why have we not been in the habit of seeing the history in this way? Presumably there is no grand conspiracy, so what can explain our amnesia in this regard? The political theorist Anthony Marx, now president of Amherst College, has provided a compelling set of reasons. Marx writes that we have been trained to forget the true history:

> Elites have purposefully encoded or advocated such selective amnesia. In the aftermath of religious wars in France, in 1570 the King's Edict of Saint-Germain declares: 'First, that the remembrance of all things past on both parts, for and since the beginning of the troubles . . . shall remain as wholly quenched and appeased, *as things that never happened*.'"[13]

13. Marx, *Faith in Nation*, 30. Emphasis mine.

After the St. Bartholomew's Day Massacre, the Royal Edict of Union declared, in July 1588, that "to render the present union permanent and lasting . . . we intend forever to bury the memory of past troubles and divisions."[14] In other words, one reason why we have accepted the standard account of the wars of religion is that we have been systematically trained to forget alternative explanations, or at least to remember selectively only that which does not call to mind the prominence of state agency as their driving force.

Anthony Marx sees Saint Bartholomew, as a result of the massacre, as the "patron saint" of nationalism. Because of Bartholomew's status, as a martyr among the twelve apostles who handed on the Catholic faith and the institution of the church, Marx views him as a "symbol" of a tensioned merger in history between this-worldly and other-worldly power. It is, from a Christian point of view, a misuse of a great saint; but that is partly the point. "If we seek now a new covering other than nationalism, we do so still carrying . . . the scars it has left."[15] Marx suggests that nationalism has faded somewhat, and with it our memories of what it has cost us. We have been trained to be amnesiacs, to forget our bloodied past. Yet he suggests that by remembering what nationalism has cost us in the past, we have a much better chance of understanding what has gone wrong and how we might resist its pull in the future.

One of the things it has cost is Christian unity. In a different context Hugo Rahner once noted that "all the

14. Potter, *French Wars of Religion*, 203, quoted in Marx, *Faith in Nation*, 30.

15. Marx, *Faith in Nation*, 206.

churches who wish to withdraw from the unity of the church dogmatically first of all seek refuge with the state but soon are absorbed by the state and fall with it."[16] From a different critical angle, historian G. R. Elton observed that "the Reformation maintained itself wherever the lay power (princes or magistrates) favoured it; it could not survive where the authorities decided to suppress it."[17] If Protestant, Catholic, and Orthodox Christians have sometimes unwittingly tied their Christianity to the nation-state, they have done so along certain set grooves in history that we too often forget.

AGAIN WITH HOBBESIAN BODIES

To return to the ancient Christian view of how human beings are united in Christ, we recall that unity in the church is a return to that original communion with God that all of humanity was meant to enjoy before the Fall. Through baptism into Christ's death, and through Christians' continual participation in Christ's life through the Eucharist that makes the Body of Christ on pilgrimage, Christians have always believed that unity can be tasted, it can be mysteriously ingested, but it cannot be grasped, only seen in the sacraments and received in prayer. Leviathan is the opposite of the Body of Christ. In the Christian political imagination, the Christian becomes more herself the more she becomes attached to Christ's Body. This is why Henri de Lubac has rightly said that "the Eucharist makes the

16. Rahner, *Church and State*, xvi.

17. Elton, "Age of the Reformation," quoted in Cavanaugh, *Theopolitical Imagination*, 26.

Church." Christians stake their existence on Christ's Body, but in the Hobbesian body, it is the sovereign state that stakes its existence on humanity. From a political point of view, the church conceives of its group life as a gift received, and the sovereign state conceives itself as a will to power, and thus must secure its existence by disciplining humanity to conform to the will of the state.

Charles Tilly has argued that this makes the politics of the modern state very much like the proverbial "protection racket" of organized crime.[18] The state requires the consent of individuals for its existence. In order to maintain this consent, however, the state must discipline individuals to continually give their will, preferably in regular cycles that renew the life of the state. The idea here is not individualism generating communalism; the idea is that passive citizens give their power to the state in exchange for protection, entirely unaware that once they have given their power, the existence of the state depends on being able to manipulate the will of the people. In a sense, the Hobbesian body is far more powerful than even the much-discussed Machiavellian one. Hobbes learned that collecting mass consent, mass sentiment, is the most efficient means of gaining power—and keeping it.

Once consent has been given, the individual is hooked. You want peace and security for your family, you want to be free to pursue your own interests, and perhaps most importantly, you want your private property, your economic interests, protected. The result, of course, is that because the "social contract" is constructed in this way, the most powerful economic interests will dictate the ends of the state.

18. Tilly, "War Making and State Making as Organized Crime."

Leviathan easily becomes a tool in the private hands of a powerfully wealthy few.

Like Luther and Machiavelli, Calvin and Hobbes are working at similar problems but from different sides of Christianity and politics. Calvin and Hobbes, however, may be more deeply at odds. Calvin clearly wants to see the state as receiving its authority from the Word of God, and Hobbes wants to see the state collect its authority from individual Christians who are now to see that their redemption from the state of nature will come from the state. The church has dropped out of the picture in a peculiar way; in the transfer, it is now the state that will save us, especially from those bloody wars of religion.

John Locke (1632–1704) attempted to make Hobbes political thought more Christian, but Locke only deepened the economic dimension of the Hobbesian contract. "Property," Locke said, was "no small tie" on people's obedience. It is no surprise then that in the Lockean views of Thomas Jefferson, a largely mercantilist vision translated the "pursuit of happiness" as the pursuit of private economic interests. Happiness had once been associated, in the early and medieval church, with the vision of God. Now happiness had been reduced to a pursuit rather than a pilgrimage. Life, liberty and the pursuit of happiness would be found through hard work and economic production.

The modern political vision of happiness, enshrined in the U.S. Constitution, while noble with respect to human dignity and the love of freedom, is also troubled. What is disturbing is that in the midst of all the transfer of power from church-society to nation-state, most Christians did not even notice that happiness had come to be associated with the accumulation of wealth. Somehow, the so-called "Protestant work ethic" had been placed in the service of the capital expansion of nations. Also aiding nation-state expansion were new ideas about the power of the masses. An old Greek word was used, but "democracy" now carried with it a whole new range of meanings.

SUGGESTED READING

Calvin, John. *The Institutes of the Christian Religion.* Nashville: Hendrickson, 2008.

Hobbes, Thomas. *Leviathan.* Oxford: Oxford University Press, 1998.

Locke, John. *Two Treatises of Government.* Cambridge: Cambridge University Press, 1988.

Marx, Anthony. *Faith in Nation.* Oxford: Oxford University Press, 2005.

Cavanaugh, William T. *Theopolitical Imagination.* London: T. & T. Clark, 2003.

EIGHT

Restless Democracy's True Desire

If Luther had his alter ego in Machiavelli's *principe*, Calvin may have had his in Thomas Hobbes's "matter, form, and power of a commonwealth ecclesiastical and civil." The mystical elements that had already shifted from the sacraments to the church, to the wider society, migrated to new ways of understanding the nature of the person, community, and history. Where the old medieval societal structure had emerged organically within the church-society, now that human beings had been detached from those structures, new frameworks were needed to unite people into meaningful communities once more. The idea of the nation-state was not an adequate framework in itself; it had to appeal to ideals, principles, and natural truths. The ideas that order our Western political imagination and form the structure for modern liberal democracy were formed out of the patterns of thinking that developed in the sixteenth and seventeenth centuries. Those patterns, as we have been discussing, began to draw on theological imagery and meaning to bolster their self-consciously secular ideas about government.

In this chapter our fundamental tasks are to identify what is true about democracy, and to ask how false notions of the *corpus mysticum* may have shaped the formation of our democratic ideal. Since these configurations of power also shape the contemporary relationship between Christianity and politics, we want to know what sort of freedom and fraternity democracy points towards.

We may think of the eighteenth century as a new "age of reason" emerging from the traumas of the violent break away from medieval culture. In fact, the eighteenth century was also an age of "revolution." As Sheldon Wolin has argued, and our history has illustrated, the philosophical tradition of "liberalism" had been "born in fear, nourished by disenchantment."[1] The anthropology of the new liberal order believed that the "the human condition was and was likely to remain one of pain and anxiety."[2] Living in Calvin's Geneva, Jean Jacques Rousseau put it most romantically, stating that "man was born free, but is everywhere in bondage."[3] According to Rousseau, the "chains" were those hierarchical structures of authority of the inherited medieval tradition that stressed obedience and duty over rights and entitlements. In light of this, revolution seemed rational. One of the most important questions we can ask in seeking to understand the relationship between Christianity and politics today was whether the new political reason emerging was really as rational as it imagined itself to be.

1. Wolin, *Politics and Vision,* 263.
2. Ibid.
3. Rousseau, *Social Contract.*

JEAN JACQUES ROUSSEAU (1712–1778)

We have given space to Ferdinand and Isabella's Spain, Luther's Germany, Machiavelli's Italy, Hobbes's England, and Calvin's Geneva. Some one hundred and fifty years after the death of Calvin, Jean Jacques Rousseau was born in that same city. Like Luther and Machiavelli, Rousseau experienced the cultural alienation that was the consequence of the unhinging of society so many years after medieval society had fragmented. "We no longer live in our own place, we live outside it," he wrote in 1762.[4] It should come as no surprise that, like Calvin, Rousseau was passionate about the *need for community.*

Rousseau accepted the Hobbesian description of humanity as a depraved animal, but he rejected the notion that this was the true nature of humanity. To be "outside" our true humanity, then, was to be alienated indeed. If we keep in mind that Rousseau had once been a Calvinist, we can see that his is a story of creation and fall that manages to both imitate and invert the Calvinist view of human depravity which had understood sin as a kind of alienation from our true humanity. In Rousseau's view, however, we are not born sinners but are born free. Depravity comes through society rather than through original sin. As Rousseau put it, "All his life long man is imprisoned by our institutions."[5] The Christian tradition, following Augustine's distinction between the social and the political, had long praised "society" over "politics." However, Rousseau argued that it was our *social institutions* that were imprisoning humanity, not sin.

4. Rousseau, *Émile*, 55.
5. Ibid., 11.

What made this sense of alienation so profound for Rousseau was that, in his view, we could never go back to that original freedom. As with Calvin's view that we cannot return to the state of nature prior to the fall, Rousseau imagines a new redemptive community constituted not by giving up freedom (as with Hobbes), but constructed out of the primordial freedom of humanity. Such sentiments recalled to mind those older Christian ideas, that "our hearts are restless" for the original freedom that humanity had in communion with God before the fall.[6] However, Rousseau cannot wait for whatever rest there may be in God, for now the transcendent frame in which medieval social and political life made sense had become fragmented. Closure to the transcendent had become possible, if not necessary.[7] Nevertheless, even if not the original freedom of peace with God, Rousseau still wanted freedom. He had been deeply influenced by Calvin's notion of the interdependence of every sphere of society under God's sovereignty as well as to the complex cooperation of spheres that Calvin believed generated society, gave it its power, its political reason, its moral conscience. Yet he was convinced that this same society was responsible for enslaving and depraving the human person "born free, but everywhere in bondage." What kind of answer to this problem could there be?

Imagine for a moment that you could be stripped of all those aspects of yourself that have been formed by "society." You are not defined by your nation, race, family, or culture. You are just the collection of atoms that you are, at peace with yourself in what a later theorist, following Rousseau,

6. Augustine *Confessions* I.1.
7. See Taylor, *Secular Age*, 541–44.

will call "the original position."[8] Rousseau thought that here, stripped of everything that makes you yourself, the human person is really free. Society only adds these endless complications of identity that impede our freedom, our desires, our reason, and our imagination. It is as if Rousseau has taken the impetus of the reformation to an extreme conclusion: the break away from the Catholic Church was the break away from the social institutions and traditions of Christianity as the social whole. Luther and Calvin could not have followed him in this line of reasoning, but they made it possible for him to arrive at the conclusion that we are most free when we are not the selves that we have become. Interestingly, the "conscience" is no longer thought to be formed in a community ordered to the truth, nor directed by Christ the inner teacher, nor can we say that he is interested in Luther's individual, "interiorized" and affective conscience. For Rousseau, conscience is not part of this original position at all, because conscience is one of those cages of society that does not lead to the freedom and peace that human beings are so restlessly directed towards. However, the instinctual need for community is very much present in Rousseau's new anthropology. Now a new community can be formed based not on the narratives and so-

8. Rawls, *Theory of Justice*. Rawls was an American moral philosopher working after the Second World War, and posthumously is considered one of the great "social contract" theorists. Rawls argued that this "original position" was necessary to arrive at an adequate account of justice. By returning to this "original position," Rawls imagined that, from behind a "veil of ignorance" concerning all of the acquired social particulars that make us who we are, we would be in the best position to make the most just decisions in our moral lives. Such a development of Rousseau clearly reveals that "conscience" in the modern period is no longer conceived of something that must be formed in community.

cial institutions of the church, but based on the raw, human need for inter-dependence and communion. The thought is revolutionary. It adds a new, passionate, democratic spark to the political thought of Machiavelli, Hobbes, and Locke. It brings a disenchanted, yet mythological focus back to the individual human person as the basis for freedom and community. For all the rationalism of such eighteenth-century social and political thought, Rousseau's passionate new anthropology provided timely reading material for revolutionaries who formed new nations. They centered their ideas on a freedom that was rooted in the so-called raw nature of the human person and her primal need for community. In such a view of anthropology we can see the personal roots of modern liberal democracy. It is worth recounting, then, how in the eighteenth century, we arrived at an anthropology that had so profoundly detached human beings from older notions of persons and community. The Eucharist had been systematically displaced from the social imagination, and the relationship between person and community had been reshaped. Something had changed in the way we imagined how we were connected to one another, and to the transcendent. Something had changed in the heart of the human subject.

The Rise and Fall of the Conscience in the New Order

The Protestant Reformers, no less than Thomas Hobbes, John Locke, and Jean-Jacques Rousseau, bequeathed to their liberal progeny "the problem of subjectivism implicit in both the Protestant belief in the primacy of individual judgment and the Hobbesian insistence that human judgments were inevitably tainted by personal bias or by interest."[9] Wolin sees the political implications clearly: "liberalism transformed the older notion of the common good from an object posited by reason to one rooted in desire."[10] This made the language of the common good work quite differently than it had in earlier times.

From the early Christian understanding of community to the medieval, a coherent view of the common good had emerged that had largely understood the conscience to be present in the human person by virtue of being created in the image of God, and that it was formed, purified, and expanded in communion with Christ. If we return to our story about the migration of the *corpus mysticum,* we see how an individualist piety around the Eucharist developed long before Luther. However, Wolin's work suggests that the "individualism" works as much in terms of moral judgments, and thus political authority, than in Eucharistic terms alone. As should be clear by now, all these terms are complexly related. Luther's sacrifice of "the political relevancy of the Christian ethic" naturally meant that the moral judgments of the community would have to be carried not by the community, but by the individualized conscience—now also detached from the Eucharist of the church catholic. Once the individual conscience was detached from community, once conscience "falls" into the individualizing tendencies of modern thought, it would not be long before conscience could be understood simply as the "desires" and "instincts"

9. Wolin, *Politics and Vision,* 297.
10. Ibid., 298.

of Rousseau's primal savage, free from social discipline—in a sense, detached from Christ's body.

On the other hand, Wolin suggests that with Calvin, and with Locke, we can see an attempt to restore that "lost" community, and thus an attempt to articulate a "collective conscience." However, the subjectivized sense of conscience that had emerged became useful for the configurations of power, and so any return to the older notion of a communally formed conscience in the life of the church was unlikely. The only way to "exteriorize" the conscience now, and thus make it genuinely collective, was to look for political arrangements that could protect what "a growingly secular society most treasured; namely, wealth and status, or more briefly, 'interests.'"[11] Wolin discerns, then, a shift from the medieval common good, to Luther's individual conscience, to Calvin's collective conscience, and finally Locke's social conscience, which is so easily transcribed to economic terms, from "personal interest" to what is in the "public interest."

By the time Rousseau bases democratic freedom on the individual freed from social constraints, the Lockean "social conscience" gives way to the need for community being expressed primarily in economic terms. For both Wolin and de Lubac, the loss of the medieval sense of community had led to a largely materialist, physicalist, and finally reductive view of the human person that could authorize inhumanity on an unprecedented scale. "Having reduced man to mere externality and stripped him of conscience, it was easy for the liberal economists to treat him as a material object," and thus property becomes the *sine qua non* for participation in

11. Ibid., 303.

the society.[12] Wolin's use of de Lubac's argument in *Corpus Mysticum* culminates in his conclusion about liberalism at the end of the first edition of *Politics and Vision*. Wolin concludes, "In retrospect the long journey from private judgment to social conformity appears as the desperate effort of liberals to fashion a substitute for the sense of community that had been lost."[13]

In sum, Wolin follows de Lubac's argument from the fourth to the thirteenth century in seeing an increasingly widespread use of the term *corpus mysticum* to describe the whole society in a way that had moved far beyond its original sacramental or ecclesial sense. However the import of Wolin's treatment of de Lubac is not only to be found in Wolin's footnotes on medieval political theology. The import of his use of de Lubac can be seen most fully in how he carries the argument further, and articulates an interpretation of the political implications of *Corpus Mysticum* that has been missing from literature on de Lubac ever since he declared his own work on the subject to be "naïve."[14] Wolin clearly did not judge de Lubac naïve, only incomplete.

With de Lubac's help, Wolin saw the significance of passages where a fifteenth century English legal theorist (such as Sir John Fortescue) would use the terms *corpus mysticum* and *corpus politicum* interchangeably to refer to either the people or the state; likewise, we can see how Jean-Jacques Rousseau's understanding of community was

12. Ibid., 306.

13. Ibid., 314.

14. De Lubac, *At the Service of the Church*, 30.

thoroughly shaped by the savage, primal, and mystical idea of a "common spirit" of "communion and dependency."[15]

Rousseau's dictum, "as soon as he is alone, man is nothing," could now be seen as merely the romantic version of the *corpus mysticum* having migrated further from its source, now generating a new theological anthropology ("Man is born free, but is everywhere in bondage"), and a new vision of the redemptive community, a social contract that protects democratic freedom, as well as spreads it as a new gospel.[16] Such migrations, in Wolin's view, would increasingly and necessarily take on nationalistic dimensions, culminating in the nineteenth-century concentrations of coercive power, namely in the newly minted nation-state. The mystical element now authorized strong notions of "a single government" in which individuals would need to make sacrifices for the distinctive identity of the political whole.

What is clear is that Wolin went historically and philosophically further than de Lubac. He understood the *corpus mysticum* argument concerning the Eucharist and also paid attention to concurrent shifts in moral philosophy. He pressed on the political implications in a way that the

15. Wolin, *Politics and Vision*, 120.

16. Cf. Cavanaugh, *Theopolitical Imagination*, 9. Cavanaugh's recent and influential argument is apparently made independently of Wolin's earlier work but the similarities are striking. Cavanaugh notes that "it is essential to see fundamental agreement between Hobbes, Rousseau, and Locke on the need to domesticate the Body of Christ in order to produce unity" (39) and "the rise of the state is predicated on the creation of the individual . . . liberated from the confines of the traditional group and now relating to other individuals on the basis of contract" (73–74).

theologian did not. Would de Lubac have moved in quite this direction? Consider de Lubac's suggestive conclusion to his argument concerning this important strand of his argument in *Corpus Mysticum:*

> In the sixteenth century, Scholastics, Humanists and Protestants spoke repeatedly of the mystical body. As an exception to this Calvin preferred to replace it with any of several analogous turns of phrase . . . But Erasmus and Luther in contrast both contributed to the success of the modern formulation. Since then, it has remained the common property of both Catholic and Protestant theologians . . . From theology it would even make some inroads into the world of philosophy: Suarez would say that people grouped into society formed: "*a mystical body that morally can be called one in itself,*" and, in his *Critique of Pure Reason,* Kant would address his readers on the *mystical body* of reasonable beings formed by the free submission of each one to the rule of moral laws.[17]

It is not unreasonable to think that Wolin's vision represents one possible political development of the trajectories that Cardinal de Lubac's early work may suggest. Moreover, while one can imagine that de Lubac would have done this work much differently, he would have found much to agree with in Wolin's development of his thesis with regard to political mysticism beyond the church. De Lubac also might have asked Wolin questions, such as, what is democracy, then? Is the new "body of the people" also tied to this new anthropology? Like the medieval king, does democracy also

17. De Lubac, *Corpus Mysticum,* 118.

have two bodies, one real and one mystical? It is to Wolin's view of democracy that we now turn.

Fugitive Democracy and the Corpus Mysticum

Wolin wants to remove the errant understanding of the *corpus mysticum* from the Western political imagination. He associates this errant understanding of the "mystical body" with the mystical power of the king or economic liberalism or the nation-state or the civil society, all political "substitutes" for the Christian communion from which they had become detached. He believes that rather than produce democracy, these institutional embodiments of liberalism have been created to discipline and manage democracy to be something other than it is from the very moment democracy erupted in eighteenth-century revolutionary France and America. Much as we have suggested that political elites were interested in constructing a Christianity that was useful to their new political ventures, Wolin argues that modern "democracy" has been similarly "managed."[18] Modern democracies are controlled reflections of "managerial, scientific, and technocratic values" that are often undemocratic and inhuman. Something has been "grafted upon" democracy that does not belong to it. In this way Wolin argues that democracy as we know it today has been distorted by the same frameworks that sought to detach the Western political imagination from the church. While liberalism understood itself as a "flight from authority," Wolin suggests that it has been in the nature of democracy to flee

18. For more on managed democracy, see Wolin, *Democracy Incorporated*.

from the manipulations of liberalism. He admits that his "unmanaged" democracy has only been successful in small pockets of local democratic action, that is, in fleeting political moments that rise up in recognition of human freedom (he thinks of the free speech movement and early civil rights activism), and he calls these democratic moments that escape managerial disciplines "fugitive." What does he mean by this?

Wolin argues that rather than accept either classical or modern accounts of democracy that reduce "democracy to a system while taming its politics by *process*," we should recognize that democracy is not a settled system. As he puts it, "The fugitive character of democracy is directly related to the fact about democracy that Aristotle emphasized: democracy's politics is the creation of those who must work, who cannot hire proxies to promote their interests, and for whom participation, as distinguished from voting, is necessarily a sacrifice."[19] Democracy, as Wolin understands it, must be radically participatory. Notice that, for Wolin, it is *work* and *sacrifice* (words with a theological memory). As he puts it, we make a category mistake by thinking of democracy "as a possible constitutional form for an entire society."[20] He sees it more in terms of temporal action than spatial arrangement. Notice then how local and "unsettled" he imagines democracy to be. Like Rousseau, he is reaching for something primordial and communal. Democracy must be direct, participatory, and radically local. What begins to emerge from such a vision is, at least in theory, like the kind of local attachments we once had in medieval

19. Wolin, *Politics and Vision*, 602.
20. Ibid.

Christendom—however, without any clear sense of what might be the organic or supernatural unity that gathers people together as a whole. Wolin has rejected liberalism for its false universalizing, and embraced democracy in all its local particularism.

While admirable in rejecting the false notions of the *corpus mysticum*, and helpful in demonstrating the ways in which liberal orders have deformed democracy, does he not eschew truth, and distort the relationship between parts and wholes in a new way? While he may free us to think afresh about democratic participation, in fear of a false whole, must this entail the rejection of any universal way of relating parts to a true whole, or to a true end? Some medieval Christians worried that Aristotle failed to discern the proper end to which the soul and the city were ordered. Perhaps a similar problem now faces us. Like Aristotle, Wolin seems to allow democracy no transcendent *telos*, no true transcendent end to which it points, no goal or purpose. In refusing ends, he also refuses the grand mysticism that he associates with the enormous scale of modern political thought. However, that means that his argument to decouple democracy and liberalism, while making us think, also remains an argument that remains closed to the transcendent. We must decide whether that closure is warranted even if we agree to refuse the false whole of political mysticism.

In his humanism, Wolin is Aristotle and Rousseau rolled into one. With Aristotle he affirms that to be human is to be political. With Rousseau he resists political forms that would restrict human beings freedom as political animals. Thus any political form that collects consent, but rejects participation, is dehumanizing. In his view, both the nation-state and the market do exactly this. His democratic project is an attractive invitation to human beings to be political agents, and to attend to their own local ways of knowing and naming the political. However, where does this leave American democratic visions of *e pluribus unum*, or other ways of imagining human solidarity such as those which transcend local or even national boundaries?

As we have seen, Wolin is critical of the liberal drive to unity, which he sees as the mystical impulse inherited from the manipulated migrations of the *corpus mysticum*. De Lubac would agree that unity is the fundamental impulse of the *corpus mysticum*. However, for Christians, unity is not solely a human labor; it is the work of the triune God who made all of humanity in his image for communion with himself. The problem of *corpus mysticum* was not its impulse for unity, the problem was in the ways the real and the mystical became detachable, and also transferable. The problems were in the ways that these migrations of the mystical body came to distort how we imagine the nature of persons and community itself. For de Lubac, the church is the city of God on pilgrimage, constantly nourished by every consecrated moment of Christ's real presence in the Eucharist that makes the church catholic, universal. Yet every consecrated moment of celebrating the Eucharist is always as radically local, and as radically participatory, as Wolin would like. Paradoxically, however, it is precisely in the local celebration of the Eucharist that the church is universal. As the saying goes, the church was never more catholic than it was in the upper room at the last supper. Would Wolin deny that this constitutes a politics, or would he merely reduce the Eucharist to the local, dismissing Christian claims to universality?

Wolin's fugitive democracy is perpetually restless by nature, not unlike Augustine's restless heart. However, rather than restless for some end to which it is called, Wolin's democracy seems restless because it must flee from the "fallen powers" that subjugate people. Wolin cannot answer, as Aristotle could not, questions about the *telos* of human souls. Aquinas himself faulted Aristotle for not being able to name the *telos* of the soul. And so we might ask, if democracy is fugitive, and we know what it is running from, what is it running towards? We know about the negative character of this restlessness, but can we say anything positively about what sort of rest to which it might be called? If democracy is on the run because it fears captivity, what would constitute its freedom from such fear? Is not democracy's fugitive "nature" itself a sign that it has lost something that would make it whole? Wolin is helpful in laying bare the restlessness of our nature as political animals, and he is right in denying that liberalism is the political form that could elevate and perfect democracy. Christians can find in him a strange ally against so many distortions, but like de Lubac, he raises more questions than he answers.

For example, how will fugitive democracy not also become totalizing, overwhelming us with the local? The problem to face here is that it is not clear that fugitive democracy can get us out of an autonomously constituted politics simply by pointing us to the local and the participatory. Even diasporic, mendicant orders within the church found that they needed concrete institutional forms of life to secure their passage across time. Though we want to agree with Wolin that the state and market are not mystical bodies, do we want to romanticize about a fugitive democracy that,

detached from all of this political mysticism, could be sufficient to resist evil on its own? From de Lubac's point of
view, only a concrete, visible church can save us—one that
finds a true, universal communion precisely in the local celebration of the Eucharist. The church catholic is local and
democratic in worship, but it is precisely in worship that it
is also beyond the local and democratic—it is universal and
even hierarchical. It is a different kind of communion, one
generated not by work or the sacrifice of human hands, but
by the person and work of Christ. Perhaps democracy is
restless for just this end?

Wolin can be seen as a political theorist who clears
a space for the political philosopher and theologian alike
to think about the political knowledge the ecclesial person
has access to through the sacramental time of the church.
Yet it must be noted that Wolin is more often right in what
he denies than what he affirms. For his critique of political mysticism is as profound as his political immanentism
is weak. Wolin reads democracy's nature rightly, at least in
part, when he views it as fugitive; but when he fails to name
properly whence that restlessness comes (fear of being
managed by the powerful), and to what end such restlessness might be rightly directed, he leads us precisely to the
questions that only theology can answer. He invites us to
take theology seriously precisely by taking us to the limits
of democratic thinking. It is in this sense that he stakes a
legitimate claim to be being the most serious political philosopher of the twentieth century.

Theologians and political philosophers' attempts to
reconcile religion and liberal democracy might look different were they to examine Henri de Lubac and Sheldon

Wolin together. Wolin wants to free democratic imaginations from the disciplines of detachment imposed by both
state and market; and he sees how political mysticism have
given both state and market a totalizing power to collect
consent and allegiance, a power that has paradoxically
stripped human beings of their political nature. In brief,
Wolin sees how dehumanizing liberal orders have been in
ways that are often reminiscent of similar concerns raised
by Christians. Henri de Lubac, on the other hand, set out to
free the ecclesial imagination from disciplines of detachment that separated the three aspects of Christ's historical
body, his sacramental-mystical body in the Eucharist, and
his true body the church. De Lubac imagined a "mystical
body politics" that was more inclusive, more humanizing,
and ultimately more social than the isolating politics of the
modern, liberal state. While Wolin cannot imagine, as de
Lubac could, a "common destiny" for the world in the true
body of Christ, he did learn from de Lubac a crucial political insight. He learned that the nationalist mystique, and its
totalitarian tendencies, is but a distorted reflection of the
corpus mysticum. Christians do well to guard themselves
from such idols (1 John 5:21).

   In conclusion, Wolin's work might be read as charged
with a divine yearning (a love, an *eros*) for that which he
cannot name. His resistance to settled political forms and
his insistence on preserving the fugitive nature of democratic action are no less cries for human freedom than
the cries of our liberal revolutionaries. Where liberalism
settled into a false mystical unity, a false "rest," Wolin's cry
for freedom resists *all* political rest through its distinctively

theological and historical argument for political struggle.[21]
As a negative political philosophy, Wolin's fugitive democracy rejects every distorted reflection of the true *corpus
mysticum*, but in resisting something false, can we see his
democracy yearning for something transcendently true? Or
do we remain trapped in a new way, in a world constituted
only by political labor? Perhaps it is true: democracy has no
transcendent end. Yet what if that is wrong? Even then we
are left with a question about the transcendent end of what
is the very basis of democracy, namely the freedom of the
human person. With all this political labor, the question of
whether there is a Sabbath for democracy becomes synonymous with whether there is a Sabbath for us.

RESTLESS DEMOCRACY'S TRUE DESIRE

Saint Augustine opened his *Confessions* with the prayer:
"You have made us for Yourself, O Lord. Our hearts are
restless until they find their rest in Thee."[22] Modern readers have often taken the prayer as a private confession, but
for Augustine it was not the cry of an individual, it was the
cry of humanity. What is attractive about Wolin's angle on
democracy is that he tells us something true about it: democracy is nothing less than restless humanity, ordinary
people who share "bits of power" so that human beings can
live decent lives. To make democracy serve the interests of
a large centralized state, or multi-national corporations,

---

21. In this respect, Wolin's localism and his agonism can be seen
as a direct rebuttal to the totalitarian implications of Carl Schmitt's
"friend-enemy" distinction in his book *The Concept of the Political*.

22. Augustine *Confessions* I.1.

is to subjugate and obscure the true nature of democracy. Like humanity itself, democracy is restless. That restlessness is a sign, Augustine tells us, of not only a political problematic in our nature, but also a theological problem. The restlessness of democracy, like the restlessness of the human heart, also signals to us that there is a peace that we all seek. The desire for human communion is writ into the fabric of democracy, a long lost memory of what humanity is destined for: participation in the truth that makes us free. In other words, the teleology that we have forgotten can also be remembered and proclaimed afresh in ways that produce a genuine Christian politics that can make the resistance of evil subordinate to the love of the good that we seek. However, such an end is not abstract, but personal and communal at once, for the *telos* that Christians name and know has been crucified, has risen and ascended to the right hand of the Father, and remains mystically and really present to humanity in the Eucharist.

When Christians are drawn together, gathered in the body of Christ through the sacrament of our unity, when we are signed with one Spirit, we have access to God in Christ. It is here that people gain a share in divine power by becoming not only members of Christ's body, but in doing so we become members one of another, where each of us shares in the good of the others. This true democracy is nothing less than the politics of "the heavenly Jerusalem in our midst." It is this body that democracy truly desires, and hopes for even in its restlessness—though it is a body that cannot be constructed, only received.

SUGGESTED READING

Lubac, Henri de. *Catholicism: Christ and the Common Destiny of Man.* San Francisco: Ignatius, 1988.

Hauerwas, Stanley, and Romand Coles. *Christianity, Democracy and the Radical Ordinary.* Theopolitical Visions. Eugene, OR: Cascade, 2007.

Rousseau, Jean-Jacques. *The Social Contract.* Oxford: Oxford University Press, 2009.

Stout, Jeffrey. *Democracy and Tradition.* Princeton: Princeton University Press, 2005.

Wolin, Sheldon. *Democracy Incorporated.* Princeton: Princeton University Press, 2008.

NINE

The Freedom of the Church

While diverse bonds of neighborly love between human beings have existed over time, only in Christ can the human
family be made truly whole. And we would argue here that
it is only in the church catholic that Christian unity can be
made visible. However, modern Christians have accepted a
settlement that weakens authentic witness to the unity of
Christ's body. The settlement has been a *political settlement*
brokered by the early modern nation-state, but accepted
by people whose intellect, imagination, memory, and conscience had been reformed and sometimes deformed
throughout the various reform movements over time.
One of the consequences of this has been that Christians
have forgotten the bonds of fraternal love that would nor-
mally order their lives, their loves, and their liberties. Many
Christians implicitly believe that there can be no argument
about the visible bonds of Christian unity because they
have also implicitly accepted the political settlement that
guaranteed any visible unity between diverse Christians
would now be provided by liberal political orders.

This book suggests that such a comprehensive political arrangement is contingent and thus not necessary. It suggests that Christian political hope is better situated around new ways of imagining the visible as well as invisible bonds of unity between Christians. Christians too often accept that we are no longer allowed to even argue hopefully (i.e., hopeful that the argument will lead us to transcendent truth) about Christian unity. The determinism that is thus attached to ecclesial division is an extension of a people who have been ordered to a unity that is political, but not a politics ordered to Christ's Body. We need to return to more hopeful modes of argument, dialogue, theological reflection, prayer, and works of charity that would lead us to modes of relation we have not yet imagined.

In this concluding chapter we consider a politics of freedom that contrasts with the kind of freedom envisioned by those who framed our modern liberal orders. In our examination of these modern accounts of political freedom, an important aspect on which we have focused has been the transformation of conscience, especially in the sixteenth and seventeenth centuries. Conscience was transformed in the name of freedom, in the name of releasing human beings from the "bondage" of tradition. In the great mystical migration, the conscience was detached and reattached to the new liberal orders. This book argues that such detachments have not made us freer. Such detachments have made us forgetful of who we are, and the tradition of which we are a part. Consequently, we struggle to identify the good that is common to us. It is difficult to know how to bring faith and political reason into mutually illuminating discourse today. If we want to return our attention to the conscience, we will have to recognize that the conscience is necessarily attached to a tradition, a living memory of the good that forms us in a virtuous community ordered to the love of the truth, goodness and beauty that we seek. In bringing this book to a close, we will need not only to sum up our narrative, but also to imagine a new course that is not simply a repetition of the past. Such a task is difficult, but try we must.

This concluding chapter has three parts (a sketch for a triptych). Indeed, each part builds upon the previous one, but each could also be taken alone as a kind of partial conclusion. In the first part we will recall the various models for relating Christianity and politics that have been surveyed in this book and ask about the ecclesial criterion for thinking in this category of relation as Christians. In the second part we will examine Pope Benedict's encyclical on Catholic social teaching, *Caritas in Veritate,* where he reflects on the priority of truth (and truthfulness) for the dialogue of faith and public reason, and for the formation of the conscience. Here we examine the conditions for forming the conscience in communion. In the wake of the history we have surveyed, it is crucial that we attend to the way God's love is concretely embodied in the practice of Eucharistic communion, and even in the papacy itself, if we want to repair the ecclesial divisions that have caused us so much pain, and have so often distorted the relation of Christianity and politics. This leads us to reflect on Benedict's vision of the papacy as "advocate of Christian memory," and as the power of the Christian conscience. Such ecumenical reflections on the papacy lead us to the call to communion where the conscience is formed and where a genuinely Christian politics of reconciliation is a witness to God's city, which abides with us even now. Rather than reflect upon this abstractly, in the third part of the conclusion we narrate a Eucharistic exchange between Pope Benedict XVI and the Metropolitan of Constantinople, Bartholomew I. In this transnational yet local narrative we witness a mode of ecclesial relation that can set our theo-political imaginations on a new course.

PART I

Models of Relating Christianity and Politics

After reading a book such as this, readers may want to reflect on the history that has been described. What does the constantly shifting relationship between Christianity and politics mean for Christians today? What does it mean for the future? How should we think of the Christian conscience, the papacy, or the Eucharist today as we seek to understand the relationship between faith and political reason, not only with a view to ecclesial unity, but also with a view to bringing the consciences of all people into an encounter with truth? As we have reflected on this history, we have viewed a number of different models for relating Christianity and politics. Ideally, we could summarize each of them in turn here, in this concluding chapter, and discuss how the church bears witness to a freedom that is distinct from the freedom of any social or political order throughout history—just as easily as we identify those moments when the church has not been entirely true to the gifts she has received. Barring a more extensive conversation about these models, let us simply review the ones we have covered by listing them as follows:

Model 1: Persecuted Minority

Model 2: Imperial Absorption

Model 3: Two Cities

Model 4: Papal Rule

Model 5: Lutheran Wedge

Model 6: Calvinist Commonality

Model 7: Hobbesian Bodies

Readers will notice that there is no distinctively Catholic or Orthodox model for the relation of Christianity and politics, though both Latin and Greek speaking Christians have clearly participated in each of these models of relating Christianity and politics over time. As well, the way we imagine the state today is reduced to a basically Hobbesian arrangement of a comprehensive social contract that is imagined to gather and protect us from a fundamental violence in nature. One can narrate the social or political whole quite differently. The models, however, are not intended to suggest a typology. Nor are the models an apologetic precursor to an account of that one perfect model (tempting as it may be, in Hegelian fashion, to construct a synthetic eighth one). There are very good reasons for why such a synthesis is not desirable, and several are worth mentioning here.

The first reason is that the only perfect model is the one that appears in the Lord's Prayer, that God's will be done "on earth as it is in heaven." That is the eschatological hope of all Christians and the end to which Christians rightly desire to direct all their actions. That is the "politics of peace" that is grounded in God's love; and the church catholic is a visible sign of this politics for the world. So to construct a synthetic model could only look utopian, inattentive to the fact that the proper relationship between Christianity and politics is eschatological.

The second reason we have not constructed a perfect, synthetic eighth model is that all but one of these models is historically contingent. That is, most of these models are not actually models but *descriptions* of real historical relations. *The only model that doesn't quite fit is the third one:* Augustine's doctrine of the two cities. It is, of course, an historical description, at least partially contingent upon the historical particulars of how Christianity and politics related in the fifth-century Roman Empire. However, this model stands apart from *mere* historical description because it is also a model conceived by a theologian who was not trying to construct a synthetic model for the relation of Christianity and politics, but who was trying to describe the *theo-political grammar* of divine revelation itself by attending to the spiritual significance of the relation between Jerusalem and Babylon that is narrated for us in the scriptures. Put differently, Augustine's narrative about the two cities is a christological rule for narrating all history. It is this third model that has endured "through the ages" (*saeculum*) and reveals the comprehensive scope of Christian thinking about politics. Indeed, *all of these models can be explained by it, but it cannot be explained by any of them.* That gives the third model a special place in shaping how we understand the freedom of the church in contrast to the more limited freedoms that can and should be secured in the contingent and temporary circumstances of time (e.g., the state as one limited association amongst many).

What such an assessment should prompt in us, however, is the realization that the fundamental task set for us in reading the history of Christianity and politics is both personal and communal. What we are asking ourselves in such a search is personal: what transcendent truth could be great enough to make the effort of my journey worthwhile? As well, we are also asking ourselves communal questions about the "whole" of which we are a part. To whom do we "belong"? These questions are ultimately questions about communion with God, but they are also questions about our neighbors and our families and how we relate to one another in what we could say were more or less good modes of relation—ways in which we can say with confidence that we are being formed in love and truth, ways in which sin can be squarely faced, ways in which forgiveness is possible. What we need in such evaluations of the personal and communal good are critical re-evaluations in the "category of relation."

Thinking in the "Category of Relation"

As we have seen, the fundamental category of relation for Christians is participation in the communion of God's triune love—visibly, mysteriously, and really present in the celebration of the Eucharist. The relation of every part to the whole is revealed in Christ whose presence is not only revealed to us in scripture, but concretely, for as we "do this in memory," we begin to conform ourselves to his presence with us. Making Christ the central criterion does not, however, displace the human person, nor negate the freedom of the will, nor destroy other categories of relation proposed by people thinking and acting in other traditions. In Pope Benedict's Christian humanism, the body of Christ reveals our true humanity and contains the personal and relational criteria for evaluating what is good in societies, cultures, and religions. Thus the pope's call to critically re-evaluate the relationship between Christianity and politics is nothing less than the call to "re-plan our journey" and to set a course towards the truth that sets free. Such a course requires modes of relating that encourage the dialogue of faith and reason, but this is not simply for the sake of dialogue.

In the modern period we have witnessed some rather corrosive ways of relating abstract notions of "religion" and "politics." The acts of terror at the World Trade Center and the Pentagon in 2001 were a tragic reminder that the relation can be very badly conceived. The slow, steady exclusion of religion from public life experienced in our modern liberal democracies received an extreme rebuke of a kind that only confirmed our wholly constructed, but all too forgetful opinion that "religion" is the cause of all our problems. In William Cavanaugh's terms, such acts only confirm "the myth of religious violence."[1] One ideology merely mirrors the other in repetitions of violence—what we observe are distorted modes of relating that are often built upon false, constructed categories (such as "religion" and "the secular"). Such exclusions of faith have resulted in further flights into irrationality.

The exclusion of religion from the public realm has hindered our ability to critically evaluate how we relate the parts to the whole, how we think about development and the good of humanity—it has also made us forgetful about the

1. See Cavanaugh, *Myth of Religious Violence*.

relationship of Christianity and politics. The ideology of the Enlightenment made it possible (even "reasonable") that we would become increasingly detached from the church, as well as from our local attachments, and that we would find ourselves attached to a new "whole," a new public in which religion had no say precisely because it was considered at best private, at worst irrational. This has not manifested the perpetual peace the Enlightenment fathers hoped that it might. Such ideologies have born some of the marks of Augustine's "city of man," most of all when they have constructed their own gods, or when they have closed themselves off from any transcendent source of goodness, or have sought the end of the good in all the wrong places. As we begin a new conversation about Christianity and politics we will need to return with patience to rethink how Christian theology contributed to the rise of the Enlightenment and to all the dominant forms of modern political order.[2]

What about the non-believer, then? What place do they have in such a new conversation? The non-believer might take comfort in the pope's affirmation that "religion always needs to be purified by reason."[3] Perhaps the atheist may hope that reason could purify religion in such a way that faith ceased to believe, or that it gave up on transcendent truth. However, that is essentially the hope to bring the dialogue of faith and political reason to a violent end. As we have seen, collapsing that relationship has been deeply

2. For one fascinating attempt at such a return for the sake of evaluating our theo-political "modes of relating" Christianity and Islam in modernity, see the work of political philosopher Gillespie, *Theological Origins of Modernity*.

3. Benedict XVI, *Caritas in Veritate*, 56.

problematic in modernity. The militant atheist and the religious fundamentalist have been poorly formed in the *same* errant modes of relation that the pope has asked us to critically reevaluate. However, the non-believer who is open to a truth that comes from beyond him has nothing to fear, except perhaps, the possibility that he is wrong—but why fear this? The most rational approach would seem to require openness to having your reasons corrected charitably and in the truth. As the pope notes, "reason always stands in need of being purified by faith: this also holds true for political reason, which must not consider itself omnipotent."[4] We need frameworks that are not theoretically closed to the transcendent, or that constantly seek to discipline religion or make it serve secular ends, but are open to a more dynamic dialogue of faith and reason. Without such frameworks that are more genuinely open to the transcendent, we are always at risk of new kinds of totalitarianism that would order us to the wrong ends. The avoidance of tyranny may thus not only depend on democratic norms, but also on transcendent ones.

That being said, Christianity does not offer political models to the world in the sense of recommending a particular arrangement of power. While the church has a specific commitment to human freedom, and thus a constitutional allergy to tyranny of any sort, the church can only offer to the world what she has been given: an encounter with God reconciling the world to himself in Christ. Christians seeking a politics, and a relationship to every other politics, will find it very near to them. As Wolin reminds us, it was not so much what Christians had to say about politics, but it was

4. Ibid.

what they had to say about their own communal life that transformed the Western political imagination. That leaves us to ask about the conditions for the formation of every conscience, and more specifically, to ask about the formation of the Christian conscience in communion. Such questions of formation are critical if we are to have any hope for the new kind of conversation about Christianity and politics we have been outlining.

PART II

The Priority of Truth and the Formation of the Conscience

The conscience, in Catholic social teaching at least, has been strongly associated with something called "natural law." This has a long, venerable tradition of Christian reflection that runs from St. Paul's interest in "the law written on the heart" to St. Augustine and St. Thomas Aquinas's fine-tuned distinctions between an *eternal law* discernible by means of metaphysical speculation, a *natural law*, discernible by observing the laws of nature, a *human law*, discernible by observing social and political arrangements, and the *divine law*, or the Old and New Testaments as God's Law, or Truth itself.

However, for some modern thinkers "natural law" does not seem so natural after all. At least we will have to admit that natural law does not seem as self-evident as it once did. It seems that conscience and natural law have followed similar paths, crisscrossing along the way over the course of the great migrations of the mystical body. Yet there is more to it than this. We now live in an intellectual climate that is highly sensitive to how human beings interact with nature and even, in an age of genetic engineering, to how they *construct nature*. We have lost a sense of nature as something that has been given to us, and so the existence of "natural law" has become less obvious. At the same time, paradoxically, and with environmental concerns mounting, we have become concerned about how our human constructions have harmed nature, and thus how something prior to us, and upon which we depend, has been eroded by us. Just as our view of the conscience became unhinged in modernity, so has our view of nature.

Added to this is the problem that, for many people, natural law, let alone eternal law, appears to be the opposite of freedom. We often do not see any good, or recognize any moral truth, that we have not constructed for ourselves. Some have suggested that we get along perfectly well without truth, or that at least we get along perfectly well without any *transcendent* truth. That is, as they say, one choice amongst many. Yet, as we have seen, it has been a problematic choice in modernity. One reason for this *theo-political* problem might be that our view of natural law has been disconnected from the two great lights of the *conscience*: metaphysical reflection on transcendent truth, and God's revelation to Israel and to the church. That is to say, we have forgotten the social location and conditions for the formation of our conscience. Another reason for this problem might be that we have been so deeply formed as participants in the "social contract," in social and political bodies of our own making (Hobbesian bodies), that we have forgotten what truly gathers us. We have either forgotten or willfully denied that there is a communion that has already been given to us, a communion that we have not simply constructed for ourselves. We have forgotten how to be formed in the truth or we have willfully denied the very possibility of being formed in the truth, and thus we have difficulty in recognizing the good that is common to us. In this sense, our theo-political problems are also personal problems for those of us formed in such orders that have forgotten that truth is not simply something we make, but truth is prior to us, given to us; truth is to be encountered and received.

This last reason animates Pope Benedict XVI's recent social encyclicals, especially *Caritas in Veritate*. In that encyclical, Benedict does not take "natural law" as the self-evident "given" as some earlier Catholic social teaching has done. Rather than make "natural law" a self-evident category, Benedict argues for the priority of truth. Why does he not argue for the self-evident nature of the good as certain natural law advocates have done, or for the priority of rights, as the liberal tradition has done? He clearly believes in natural law, and stresses both the rights and the duties due to the dignity of every human being. But he places a special emphasis on truth because without truth it is not at all clear that we can learn to become intelligible to one another about such questions that concern the common good.

The Pope implicitly admits that humans create the conditions for human flourishing. Our creative aspect for making the world is, in part, what it means to have been made in the image of God. But the Pope also argues that "without truth" humanity will lose its way in the illusion that reality is *reducible* simply to what we make it. Without truth, we forget the "natural law" written on the human heart, which, as Augustine writes, "not even iniquity itself destroys."[5] Detached from any dialogue with metaphysical and revealed transcendent truth, we fear that human laws are inevitably arbitrary, rooted only in the fleeting fancies of corporate desires (the will to power made legal). This is why Benedict laments that it often seems that "our conscience can no longer distinguish what is human, and what is good."[6] If we are looking for something that we can all hold in common with our neighbors, the pope counsels that we must first turn to face transcendent truth, for without truth it is difficult to recognize what is natural and good. The notion of the conscience, whose rise and fall we have studied, is worth revisiting in light of the Pope's counsel because we need to ask ourselves afresh questions about how we recognize the good, and what will aid our conscience in doing so. Such questions are important for all people, but given the history we have covered, it is a question that is particularly acute for Christians whose conscience was harmed by ecclesial divisions and the mystical migrations we have covered in this book. It is acute because it concerns how we participate in Christ's body.

Shepherd of Conscience

As we have noted, conscience might seem like an impediment to our freedom because we think of it as some external law, coercively imposed upon us from without, like

5. Augustine *Confessions* II.9.
6. Benedict XVI, *Caritas in Veritate,* 75.

one of Rousseau's social constraints. Luther's individualized conscience was an attempt to remedy his own sense that the church had become too beholden to juridical principles of the catholic hierarchy. And as we saw, Calvin immediately recognized that Luther had cut off the human person from the body of Christ in whom the conscience is formed. In the wake of the Enlightenment—and its new voluntaristic configurations for the formation of individual conscience—we have forgotten the ends to which the conscience is directed and the ecclesial location of its formation. In this sense, we have not only forgotten the conscience, we have forgotten the communion to which it has been called.

Benedict stresses that the conscience is a *memory of the good* implanted within us. However, without openness to transcendent truth, our desire for the good and our ability to perform the good is at least incomplete or frustrated by our forgetfulness of "that which is prior to us and constitutes us."[7] Likewise, while it is true that our conscience is instilled within us, "written on the heart," *it needs help from without.* The question is not only about the need for transcendent truth, or the need for God in forming the conscience, but also the need for a communion that is ordered to the worship of the triune God. This was the true intention of both Luther and Calvin, who each wanted in their own ways to reconnect our conscience with this new law of freedom, this gospel of grace, the new politics inaugurated in Christ. However, in their search for a more genuinely communal Eucharist, they were swept into unintended corners by political winds that frustrated their true aims. The results made it difficult for the Christian conscience confused by

7. Benedict XVI, *Caritas in Veritate,* 52.

the fragmentation of the communion in which it was made
to receive. The unity of the Eucharist was not recognized
and the sacramental nature of the papacy was sometimes
obscured by the machinations of "the city of man," or a
politics which constantly tempts humanity to grasp as pos-
session what it only rightly receives as gift.

In light of the medieval and early modern history we
have covered in this book, then, it should not be entirely surprising that in his teaching on the conscience Pope Benedict
seeks to repair our understanding of the authority of the
Petrine office as shepherd of conscience. Though it will be
controversial to say so, it is clear that Christian divisions
will not be healed without frank recognition of the failures
of the Christian imagination when it comes to the successor
of Saint Peter.[8] Consider with ecumenical patience, then,
Benedict's view of the charism of his own office:

> The true sense of the teaching authority of
> the pope consists in his being the advocate of
> Christian memory. The pope does not impose
> from without. Rather, he elucidates the Christian
> memory and defends it . . . All power that the
> papacy has is power of conscience . . . which
> again and again must be purified, expanded, and
> defended against the destruction of memory that
> is threatened by a subjectivity forgetful of its own

8. Though Martin Luther famously objected to the papacy as a
providentially ordered gift for the unity of the church catholic, it is no
longer clear that Lutherans, or any other Protestant Christians, need be
bound by such sixteenth-century contextual concerns. For one well-
known re-evaluation of the papacy from a Lutheran perspective, see
Lindbeck, "Lutherans and the Papacy," and "Papacy and *Ius Divinum,*
A Lutheran View." Also see Long, "Protestants and the Papacy," 10–11.

foundation, as well as by the pressures of social
and cultural conformity.[9]

Such a view of the papacy in the light of conscience is
fascinating given the complex history of papal power and
the subsequent rise and fall of the conscience. Rather than
following the model of Gregory VII, or others who would
have unwittingly mimicked temporal power, "forgetful of
its own foundation," Pope Benedict assumes Gregory the
Great's servant vision, or better, Saint Peter's own vision of
himself as shepherd, and as one who tells Paul to "remember
the poor." Rather than seeing the hierarchy of the church as
a highly centralized and "managed" structure, he brings our
understanding of the papacy into a fraternal framework (as
we shall see). Bearing witness to the truth as an advocate of
Christian memory, the Pope calls us to a holistic vision of
the Christian communion in which our conscience can be
formed. The visible unity that the papacy embodies is thus
not reduced to a "structure of power" that is merely external
to us, and to which we are bound by giving up our freedom,
but is seen as a visible and spiritual bond that bears witness
to our true communion as he constantly reminds us that
transcendent truth has also come to dwell with us in Christ,
God with us.

In light of the history we have covered, however, it is
clear that the relationship between Christianity and politics has been painful at times. Even the suggestion that the
successor of Saint Peter is a universal shepherd of conscience will raise the eyebrows of some Christians nearly
five hundred years after the dawn of the reformation. To

9. Benedict XVI, *On Conscience*, 22.

some it could seem that we have suggested that the pope is the single deliverer of truth, or that only Christians in communion with the successor of Saint Peter are formed in the truth. Christ's Body is more complex than either of these suggestions. All the same, is it possible that, precisely as "advocate of Christian memory," the pope can be embraced by all Christians? Perhaps Benedict's vision of the papacy can be helpful as we learn to recover a comprehensive Christian vision for how all Christians are gathered in Christ. In this way, Pope Benedict, as shepherd of Christian memory, can exemplify the way for all Christians to set a new course, not only for conscience, but also for Christian communion.

The Call to Communion and the Politics of Reconciliation

As we have said, it is the vocation of the church to bear witness to this communion. The freedom of this communion, however, does not negate what French revolutionaries proclaimed from the depths of their consciences, "*liberté, equalité,* and *fraternité,*" but it gives these cries greater depth, and re-directs them towards a more perfect freedom and fraternity. In this sense, we can agree with Henri de Lubac, that the church receives from God the "power for liberation" for the whole of humanity, the "one effective guarantee of spiritual liberty."[10] Our reasoned revolutionaries could fashion the liberal state and market, they could form a civil society, and they could expand our imaginative horizons for who we recognize as our neighbor. They exercised their political reason with great prowess, but ultimately they

---

10. De Lubac, *Splendor of the Church,* 171

produced a reductive vision of the person, and wed their political reason to violence. Pope Benedict asks,

> Will it ever be possible to obtain brotherhood by human effort alone? As society becomes ever more globalized, it makes us neighbors but does not make us brothers. Reason, by itself, is capable of grasping the equality between men and of giving stability to their civic coexistence, but it cannot establish fraternity. This originates in a transcendent vocation from God the Father, who loved us first, teaching us through the Son what fraternal charity is.[11]

That is also to say that the Eucharist gathers humanity differently than the social contract as it is expressed in Hobbes, Locke, Rousseau, and others. Rather, the Eucharist invites us to a politics that does not reduce human beings, but frees humanity for communion with God and neighbor in truth and love. Any configuration of power that is fundamentally closed (or even hostile) to this politics will inevitably find that it cannot guarantee human freedom. Rousseau's democratic sense of a primordial communion between human beings in the general will—his perceived need for a community constituted out of human freedom— was a desire for freedom that had in fact constructed a religion of humanity. This in turn actually reduced humanity by cutting human beings off from the external source of our freedom as creatures. In his search to liberate a new humanity, Rousseau's democratic ideals remained unhinged, fugitive, and restless at their core.

11. Benedict XVI, *Caritas in Veritate*, 19.

Yet it is not only a political reason closed to the transcendent that has reduced humanity. As we have seen, Christians have also been culpable in forming cities that look all too similar to Augustine's city of man: fratricidal rather than fraternal. What we have called failures of the Christian imagination we might just as well call sin. Or perhaps it is better to say that it is the consequences of sin that have weakened our desire and imaginative vision, giving rise to vicious cycles that have divided the church from within as well as from without, and have made it more difficult to locate the communion in which our consciences are most free. Consequently, confusion about the conscience, as well as confusion about communion, has made Christian claims less believable. However, fresh ecumenical winds are blowing. Let me provide one such witness to this politics of reconciliation between East and West—a witness that also helps us to rethink the place of the papacy, the Eucharist, Christian fraternity, the transnational character of the church, and, as if by accident, the relationship between Christianity and politics.

PART III

True Pax Romana

Inaugurating the year of St. Paul in 2008, Pope Benedict XVI met with Orthodox Patriarch Bartholomew I of Constantinople. These two Archbishops celebrated the Feast of Apostles Peter and Paul in St. Peter's Basilica—that is, a Eucharistic Feast—and both delivered significant homilies reflecting on the respective missions of Peter and Paul, whose relationship has always held so much significance for Catholic-Orthodox relations.[12] It is significant that Peter and Paul met in Rome, and that they were both martyred in Rome. Both men stressed that whatever their differences, the martyrdoms of Peter and Paul revealed their fundamental unity in Christ, a unity still made visible today in the celebration of the Eucharist on such an important feast day. Patriarch Bartholomew I, especially, stressed how Peter and Paul had become brothers in their martyrdom, and how in Orthodox icons they are often portrayed exchanging a "holy kiss." The Orthodox patriarch reflected on how, in celebrating the Feast of the Apostles Peter and Paul, that holy kiss is shared once more as a *witness to all people*.

In thinking further about this witness to all people that Bartholomew had pronounced in the holy kiss between Paul and Peter as a holy kiss between East and West, Pope Benedict asked why each Apostle went to Rome. Why meet in Rome? What is it about Rome that mattered to these two great apostles of the faith? And why does it still matter today? The pope writes that, for Paul:

> Rome was a stopping place on the way to Spain, in other words—according to his conception of the world—on his way to the extreme edge of the earth. He considers his mission to be the fulfillment of the task assigned to him by Christ, to take the Gospel to the very ends of the world. Rome lay on his route. Whereas Paul usually went to places where the Gospel had not yet been proclaimed, Rome was an exception. He found there a Church whose faith was being talked about across the world. Going to Rome was part of the univer-

12. Benedict XVI, Homily.

sality of his mission as an envoy to all peoples. The way that led to Rome, to which already prior to his external voyage he had traveled inwardly with his Letter, was an integral part of his duty to take the Gospel to all the peoples—to found the catholic or universal Church. For him, going to Rome was an expression of the catholicity of his mission. Rome had to make the faith visible to the whole world, it had to be the meeting place of the one faith.[13]

For Paul, the catholicity of the church was intimately tied to a concrete, particular, visible city. It was the visible meeting place of the one faith that was being talked about across the world. The locality and particularity of Rome's visibility was not at odds with the universality and catholicity of the church, indeed, it was the very sacrament, or visible sign of this sacred, spiritual universality. In his Letter to the Romans, Paul thus understands that his mission in Christ is to "win obedience from the Gentiles" so that the whole of the human world will become the worship of God.[14] As the pope reflects on Paul's meaning, he notes how *liturgical* Paul's mission is: "When the world in all its parts has become a liturgy of God, when, in its reality, it has become adoration, then it will have reached its goal and will be safe and sound."[15] Thus we are led to see Rome as a visible sign of what is invisibly and organically happening in a global and distributive way in the worship of triune God everywhere.

With Paul's reason for going to Rome is clear, the Pope asks, why did Peter go to Rome? Why not stay in Jerusalem?

13. Benedict XVI, Homily.

14. Rom 15:18.

15. Benedict XVI, Homily.

Given the history of Christianity and politics we have covered, and the argument that has been suggested throughout, the pope's answer to this question of why Peter went to Rome is instructive:

> St Peter's journey to Rome, as representative of the world's peoples, comes especially under the word "*one*": his task was to create the *unity* of the *catholica,* the Church formed by Jews and pagans, the Church of all the peoples. And this is Peter's ongoing mission: *to ensure that the Church is never identified with a single nation, with a single culture or with a single State but is always the Church of all;* to ensure that she reunites humanity over and above every boundary and, in the midst of the divisions of this world, *makes God's peace present,* the reconciling power of his love.[16]

That is a good summary of the upshot of this book as well. Peter goes to Rome not in order to identify the church catholic with a single nation, culture or state, but to be the concrete, visible unity of "the Church of all the peoples," the presence of God's peace and reconciling love. In other words, "Rome" should not be imagined to be a source of ecclesial division or a constitutive alliance with any particular nation, society, culture, or state. As we have seen, that way of imagining the hierarchy of the church catholic has been constructed in a way that distorts the very purposes of both Peter and Paul's mission—which were the purposes of a communion that transcends the divisions of this world, yet is also present in charity and in truth.

16. Benedict XVI, Homily. Emphasis mine.

It is also not accidental that such a reflection emerged precisely in the celebration of the Eucharist, God's peace made present in Christ's Body. If we recall that Peter was the first bishop of Rome, and that according to tradition his brother Andrew was the first bishop of Constantinople, we can appreciate the depth of this truth: Benedict and Bartholomew stand as men who are not simply neighbors, but are more genuinely human for being made brothers in Christ.

Perhaps the greatest witness to all people will be in the ways that Christians reconcile and heal their divisions as a light that reflects the great light of Christ crucified. As we have seen, such disunity has often been caused by what can only be called, in Augustine's sense, "the city of man." If the flight from God can be seen as irrationality, then it is the turn towards God's embrace in communion with Christ's Body that we embrace truth—and thus rationality—itself. This is the truth that Pope Benedict points us towards in both his celebration of the Eucharist and in the holy kiss between himself and Bartholomew. The good news is that this truth that we embrace also embraces us, comprehends us, and awakens our memory and conscience to recognize what is good and beautiful. In responding to this call to communion, we also receive within us the very criteria for judging every relation between part and whole. We make a journey of freedom in which we are not simply being formed by constructed visions of how we are gathered together as human beings, but we are formed in the reconciling love of Christ, in whom we remember the good more truly, and in whom we receive a unity not solely of our own making.

A Truth-Following Conclusion

This book has offered readers a brief guide to a history that is immensely complex. It can do little more than point towards some of the events that are crucial for understanding the relationship between Christianity and politics. We have left too many practical considerations untouched; we have remained silent on too many crucial historical, political, and theological issues. This has been a somewhat hurried journey out of Bethlehem, but one that I hope has brought us closer to the truth that is both near us and also beyond us.

In closing, I am reminded of how the Magi once arrived in the city of Jerusalem. They were following a star plain for all to see. What those wise men saw in that star was a sign of a great cosmic event: the birth of a king, the long-awaited king of the Jews, the Messiah (see Matthew 2). As Pope Benedict XVI put it, "the star and the sacred Scriptures were the two lights that guided the way of the Magi, who appear to us as models of genuine seekers of truth."[17] They were men of science, men of learning who were constantly looking to the heavens, receptive to the revelation of transcendent truth. They held in perfect unity intelligence and faith.

As they arrived in Jerusalem, they asked Herod, the king of the Jews in Jerusalem, "where is he who has been born king of the Jews? For we have seen his star in the East, and have come to worship him" (Matt 2:2). The sacred scriptures were opened up to them, and they listened to the prophecies of Israel that said: from "Bethlehem . . . shall

17. Benedict XVI, *Angelus*.

come a ruler who will govern my people Israel" (Matt 2:6). Making their way to Bethlehem they saw the star again, which the Pope has interpreted as "a confirmation of the perfect harmony between human seeking and divine Truth, a harmony that filled the hearts of these genuine wise men with joy."[18] They had come to the end of their search, finding the child Jesus with his mother. The Gospel says "they fell down and worshiped him" (Matt 2:11).

Pope Benedict ends his *angelus* following the celebration of the Mass on the Feast of the Epiphany with this thought:

> It would have been natural to return to Jerusalem, to Herod's palace and the Temple, to proclaim their discovery. Instead, the Magi, who chose the Child as their sovereign, protected him in concealment, in keeping with Mary's style, or better, with that of God himself. And thus, as they appeared, they disappeared in silence, content, but also changed by the encounter with Truth. They had discovered a new face of God, a new royalty: that of love.[19]

This is the genuinely Christian politics, being changed in "the encounter with Truth," and formed in the communion of God's triune love which is poured out for humanity in the incarnation, on the cross of Christ, and through his bodily resurrection. The freedom of the church catholic consists precisely in this communion. In thinking through the complex relationship of Christianity and politics, the Magi are genuine models of truth-seeking for us as well.

18. Benedict XVI, *Angelus*.
19. Ibid.

On their journey they used both intelligence and faith, and found the true sovereign in the human face of God.

SUGGESTED READING

Benedict XVI. *Caritas in Veritate*. Washington, DC: USCCB, 2009.

———. *Church, Ecumenism, and Politics*. San Francisco: Ignatius, 2008.

Benedict XVI, and Jürgen Habermas. *The Dialectics of Secularization: On Reason and Religion*. SanFrancisco: Ignatius, 2007.

Benedict XVI, and Marcello Pera. *Without Roots: The West, Relativism, Christianity, Islam*. New York: Basic, 2006.

Bibliography

Aristotle. *Nichomachean Ethics.* Translated by David Ross. Oxford: Oxford University Press, 1998.

———. *The Politics and the Constitution of Athens.* Cambridge: Cambridge University Press, 1996.

Augustine. *Essential Sermons.* The Works of Saint Augustine. Translated by Edmund Hill. New York: New City, 2007.

———. *Retractions.* The Fathers of the Church. Washington, DC: Catholic University of America Press, 1999.

———. *The City of God.* Translated by Henry Bettenson. London: Penguin Classics, 2003.

Bammel, Ernst, and C. F. D. Moule. *Jesus and the Politics of His Day.* New York: Cambridge University Press, 1984.

Benedict XVI. *Angelus* on the Feast of the Epiphany, January 6, 2010. Online: http://www.vatican.va/holy_father/benedict_xvi/angelus/2010/documents/hf_ben-xvi_ang_20100106_epifania_en.html.

———. *Caritas in Veritate.* Washington, DC: USCCB, 2009.

———. *Church, Ecumenism, and Politics.* San Francisco: Ignatius, 2008.

———. *In the Beginning: A Catholic Understanding of Creation and the Fall.* Grand Rapids: Eerdmans, 1995.

———. *On Conscience.* San Francisco: Ignatius, 2007.

Benedict XVI, and Bartholomew I. Homily at the Holy Mass on the Solemnity of the Holy Apostles Peter and Paul, *Vatican Basilica,* June 29, 2008. Online: http://www.vatican.va/holy_father/benedict_xvi/homilies/2008/documents/hf_ben-xvi_hom_20080629_pallio_en.html.

Benedict XVI, and Jürgen Habermas, *The Dialectics of Secularization: On Reason and Religion.* San Francisco: Ignatius, 2007.

Benedict XVI, and Marcello Pera. *Without Roots: The West, Relativism, Christianity, Islam.* New York: Basic, 2006.

Boniface VIII. *Unam sanctam*. Papal Bull, promulgated November 18, 1302. Online: http://www.fordham.edu/halsall/source/b8-unam .html.

Bossy, John. "The Mass as a Social Institution." *Past and Present* 100 (1983) 29–61.

Braaten, Carl E., and Robert W. Jenson, editors. *Union with Christ: The New Finnish Interpretation of Luther*. Grand Rapids: Eerdmans, 1998.

Calvin, John. *The Institutes of the Christian Religion*. 2 vols. Nashville: Hendrickson, 2008.

Cavanaugh, William T. *The Myth of Religious Violence: Secular Ideology and the Roots of Modern Conflict*. Oxford: Oxford University Press, 2009.

———. *Theopolitical Imagination: Discovering the Liturgy as a Political Act in an Age of Global Consumerism*. Edingurgh: T. & T. Clark, 2003.

Dawson, Christopher. *The Dividing of Christendom*. San Francisco: Ignatius, 2008.

Dodaro, Robert. *Christ and the Just Society in the Thought of Augustine*. Cambridge: Cambridge University Press, 2008.

Duffy, Eamon. *Saints and Sinners: A History of the Popes*. New Haven: Yale University Press, 2002.

Figgis, John Neville. *Political Thought from Gerson to Grotius: 1414–1625*. New York: Harper, 1960.

Gillespie, Michael Allen. *The Theological Origins of Modernity*. Chicago: University of Chicago Press, 2008.

Hauerwas, Stanley, and Romand Coles. *Christianity, Democracy and the Radical Ordinary: Conversations Between a Radical Democrat and a Christian*. Theopolitical Visions. Eugene, OR: Cascade, 2007.

Hayes, Carlton J. H. *Nationalism: A Religion*. New York: Macmillan, 1960.

Hobbes, Thomas. *Leviathan*. Oxford: Oxford University Press, 1998.

Kantorowicz, Ernst. *The King's Two Bodies: A Study of Medieval Political Theology*. Princeton: Princeton University Press, 1997.

Lindbeck, George. "Lutherans and the Papacy." *Journal of Ecumenical Studies* 13 (1976)

———. "Papacy and *Ius Divinum*, A Lutheran View." In *Papal Primacy and the Universal Church*. Edited by Paul C Empie and T. Austin Murphy. Minneapolis: Augsburg, 1974.

Livy. *Early History of Rome*. Books I–V. London: Penguin, 2002.

Locke, John. *Two Treatises of Government*. Cambridge: Cambridge University Press, 1988.

Lohfink, Gerhard. *Jesus and Community: The Social Dimension of Christian Faith*. Translated by John P. Galvin. Minneapolis: Fortress, 1984.

Long, D. Stephen. "Protestants and the Papacy: In Need of a Pope?" *Christian Century*, May 17, 2005, 10–11.

Lubac, Henri de. *At the Service of the Church: Henri de Lubac Reflects on the Circumstances that Occasioned His Writings*. San Francisco: Ignatius, 1993.

———. *Catholicism: Christ and the Common Destiny of Man*. San Francisco: Ignatius, 1988.

———. *Corpus Mysticum: The Eucharist and the Church in the Middle Ages*. London: SCM, 2006.

———. *The Splendor of the Church*. San Francisco: Ignatius, 1999.

Luther, Martin. *Luther: Selected Political Writings*. 1974. Reprinted, Eugene, OR: Wipf & Stock, 2003.

Machiavelli, Niccolo. *The Prince*. Oxford: Oxford University Press, 2008.

Marx, Anthony. *Faith in Nation: Exclusionary Origins of Nationalism*. Oxford: Oxford University Press, 2005.

Mendels, Doron. *The Rise and Fall of Jewish Nationalism: Jewish and Christian Ethnicity in Ancient Palestine*. Anchor Bible Reference Library. New York: Doubleday, 1992.

Miller, Maureen. *Power and the Holy in the Age of the Investiture Conflict*. New York: Bedford/St. Martin's, 2005.

O'Daly, Gerard. *Augustine's City of God: A Reader's Guide*. Oxford: Oxford University Press, 2004.

Pecknold, C. C. "Migrations of the Host: Fugitive Democracy and the Corpus Mysticum." *Political Theology* 17:1 (2010) 77–101.

Plato. *The Republic*. Translated by Tom Griffith. Edited by G. R. F. Ferrari. Cambridge Texts in the History of Political Thought. Cambridge: Cambridge University Press, 2000.

Prodi, Paolo. *The Papal Prince. One Body and Two Souls: The Papal Monarchy in Early Modern Europe*. Cambridge: Cambridge University Press, 1982.

Rahner, Hugo. *Church and State in Early Christianity*. San Francisco: Ignatius, 1992.

Rawls, John. *A Theory of Justice*. Cambridge, MA: Belnap, 1971.

Rousseau, Jean-Jacques. *Émile*. North Clarendon, VT: Tuttle, 1993.

———. *The Social Contract*. Oxford: Oxford University Press, 2009.

Schmitt, Carl. *Political Theology: Four Chapters on the Concept of Sovereignty.* Chicago: University of Chicago Press, 2006.

Steinmetz, David. *Luther in Context.* Grand Rapids: Baker, 2002.

Stout, Jeffrey. *Democracy and Tradition.* Princeton: Princeton University Press, 2005.

Taylor, Charles. *A Secular Age.* Boston: Harvard University Press, 2007.

Tierney, Brian. *The Crisis of Church and State 1050–1300.* Toronto: University of Toronto Press, 1988.

Tilly, Charles. "War Making and State Making as Organized Crime." In *Bringing the State Back In*, edited by Peter B. Evans, Dietrich Rueschemeyer, and Theda Skocpol, 169–91. Cambridge: Cambridge University Press, 1985.

Weber, Max. *The Protestant Ethic and the Spirit of Capitalism.* London: Penguin, 2002.

Wolin, Sheldon. *Democracy Incorporated: Managed Democracy and Inverted Totalitarianism.* Princeton: Princeton University Press, 2008.

———. *Politics and Vision: Continuity and Innovation in Western Political Thought.* Princeton: Princeton University Press, 2006.